THE 3rd DAY

(The Spirit Of Revelation)

Apostle Don Hughes
Dr. (Prophet) Tim Hines

The 3rd Day (Spirit of Revelation)
ISBN 1-931600-17-1
Copyright © 2004 by
Impact Church
Apostle Don Hughes
Dr. (Prophet) Tim Hines
P.O. Box 691563
Charlotte, North Carolina 28227-7027

Published by IMPACT Church
Apostle Don Hughes
Dr. (Prophet) Tim Hines
P.O. Box 691563
Charlotte, North Carolina 28227-7027

ENDORSEMENTS

This book will fill in the blanks for you prophetically, and help you better understand why your own personal destiny demanded that you live to witness the dawn of the 21st Century. This is the greatest time in human history to be alive, and Apostle Don Hughes and Prophet Tim Hines have definitely located the pulse and heartbeat of the Body of Christ *in the now*, opening up a door of revelation through which you can freely flow into your own purpose within Christ.

> Bishop Jim Earl Swilley
> Church In The Now
> Now Ministries
> Conyers, Georgia

Truthful, anointed, powerful! This book needs to be read again and again. Every once in awhile I read a book that I wish I had written. This book is definitely one of them!

> Dr. Don Hughes (Sr.)
> Don Hughes Ministries
> Church Alive
> Broken Arrow, Oklahoma

The Body of Christ should be established in the truth of sound doctrine (Colossians 1:23). But also in the present truth that God is prophetically emphasizing at the time (2 Peter 1:12). The present truth as revealed in the "3rd Day" is one of the most powerful truths being revealed to the Body of Christ in these last days. Don Hughes and Tim Hines give a unique apostolic and prophetic insight that the church needs to understand. I highly recommend this book to anyone who desires to know what the Spirit is saying to the church in this last hour.

Pastor David Garcia
Brooksville A/G (Home of the Grace Dome)
Brooksville, Florida

Iron Sharpens Iron and that is what I admire about my son in the faith, Tim Hines. As long as I can recall, Tim has been an individual to ignite change in those he comes in contact with. This book is an inspiration to those who have always known there was something different about how they worship, how they praise, and how they felt about their Lord and Savior. These "servants" have gone beyond the NORM and there is a people in the Lord that men and women like Tim must bring together. With this cutting edge message for these days, there will be a riot in the land, a righteous invasion of truth. Juanita and I, are so blessed to have had a part in Tim's life with the good, bad, ugly, there is "NO FLUFF" in him. You will be blessed as you read this uncompromising pivotal message.

If you don't want to change, this book isn't for you, but as for me and my household, we are a "3rd DAY" generation.

Pastor Isaac and Juanita Nunez
Heritage Family Fellowship
Porterville, California

The Day of the Lord begins in the evening and ends in the morning (Gen. 1:5). We don't see all things clearly, yet the path of the righteous is shining ever more brightly (Prov. 4:18). God has graciously given His Word to light our path (Psa. 119:105). He has opened His Word to our understanding, and continues to raise up fresh voices to articulate His mind and purpose. My friend, Apostle Don Hughes from Charlotte, North Carolina, is one of the men in our state and region whose voice the Lord has anointed to speak forth "present truth" (2 Pet. 1:12), to a new generation of men and women. We are living in unprecedented days of manifest glory. This is the Day of the Lord, the seventh day from Adam and the "third day" from Jesus (Hos. 6:1-3; 2 Pet. 3:18). This latest work from Don will help many to freshly understand this "kairos" moment, this opportune season of the Kingdom. May you be blessed and strengthened to move forward with the Lord as you read this volume from one of God's anointed vessels.

Dr. Kelley Varner
Praise Tabernacle Ministries
Richlands, North Carolina

Dedication
Apostle Don Hughes

First of all, to my parents, Dr. Don & Karrel Hughes Sr. Dad and Mom, your example of "Godly" is one of the best I have ever seen. Your relentless pursuit of the things of God and passion to help the people of God is the catalyst that prepared me for ministry. Dad, thanks for mirroring before me the "importance of" studying God's word as well as the "how to." Much of the revelation I am receiving today, I believe is the result of your labor. Dad, thank you for teaching me to selflessly give yourself to your calling. I am proud to call you, Dr. Don Hughes Sr., my dad, mentor and friend in the Kingdom. Mom, you allowed Dad to travel the world to answer his call and fulfill his destiny. You are one of the most giving women I know. Your example of "unconditional" love for your children, always putting our needs above your own, loving us through the pains of adolescence (you know! skipping school to go fishing, stealing blank report cards to change my terrible grades, wrong choices in girl friends, etc.). You worked full time, raised four children, and always had a "listening ear" to hear my latest fiasco. You truly have a pastor's heart and I am grateful that I came from you.

Secondly, my wife and co-laborer in the Kingdom, Leesa Hughes. Honey, your zeal for God and your passion for His presence often brings me to conviction. God knew what I needed when He gave me you! Someone who loves deeply, forgives often, and one who will never be found in mediocrity. You said "we can" when most said "we can't", you said "God said" when others were saying "that can't be God." You said "if we will just pray and agree...watch and see." WOW!!! That's what you are, a W...oman O...f the W...ord. From the depths of my heart, thank you for allowing me to go to the nations with the message God has given me. You are "one of a kind" and I am honored that you are mine.

Finally, to my grandson Caleb Aaron Grayson Hughes (the only grandchild at the writing of this book). Nana and I love you greatly and enjoy our Friday nights with you at "Papa & Nana's" house. Going to Papa's store (Sam's), taking you to the latest children's movies and actually enjoying it (I never thought that I would hear myself confess that), eating popcorn and candy (without your parents knowing...well they do now) and playing with "Thomas the Train." Being with you brings life to me. I was so young when my children were born that I think I missed a lot. God gave me another chance with you. I pray that you never have to experience many of the things your Papa has gone through. Serve God all the days of your life and His best will be yours. I love you little "munchkin"!

Dedication
Dr. (Prophet) Tim Hines

I want to dedicate this project to my family. To my wife Jodi, my daughter Moriah, and my son Nathan. They truly are the most important people in my life.

To my wife Jodi, my best friend, my co-laborer in the work of the kingdom. You are the fulfillment of my heart. You are dedicated to our family's success in ways that are indescribable. You live a very sacrificial life that enables us to stay together on the road, and for that I can't thank you enough. You allow me time with the Lord when you could demand that time to be with you. Because of whom you are, and all that you are inclined to do, I will spend the rest of my life loving you, and trying to serve you with all my heart. Thank you babe, you're the best.

To my daughter Moriah, my hand maiden of the Lord. I love all that you are. Happy, good natured, funny, creative, and full of life. You are my "sunshine", when you walk into a room, the atmosphere changes. I love the way that you love the Lord. For your willingness to travel from state to state and share the gospel. I will always pray the prayer that the Lord gave to us for you the day that you were born. The Lord said, "Pray that I place her in touch with my plan at an early age." You have the heart of a servant in ways that are simply supernatural. You are irreplaceable, and as you grow in years, the body of Christ will see who you are. They will enjoy what I get to enjoy every day of my life.   Moriah, I love you, we will spend our life together serving the Lord.

To my little prophet in the making, Nathan. You are strong, fearless and reckless in the call of life and the work of the Kingdom. Your passion to preach at the age of eight absolutely amazes me. I love your zeal for the upward call of God.   Your desire to worship, pray, and pray for the sick with me is an honor to labor with. You're witty and creative nature is a great comfort and blessing to be around. You are my "man of God" and I will do my best to lead you in the ways of righteousness. You went on the road at the age of five weeks old, the ministry way of life is all that you know. I pray that this special way of life is all that you ever know. I love you son, and I look forward to what the Lord will allow us to accomplish together for His glory.

Acknowledgements

To the **"servant team"** pastors of Impact Church, Byron & Tiffani Bacon, Ken & Glenda Hardeo, Curtis & Renee Davenport, Doug & Janet Wellmon and Evangelist Arnold & Holly Taylor for your understanding of **"team"** ministry. Your faithfulness to the vision and your loyalty to Pastor Leesa and I allows us to fulfill the apostolic call on our lives. We couldn't affectively go to the nations, accomplish everything on our **"plate"** without your sacrifice along side of us. As you have become well aware of; ministry is rarely **"convenient"** and yet you persevere right there with us. Pastor Leesa and I love you and there is "nothing you can do about it." Always remember:

For God [is] not unrighteous to forget your work and labour of love , which ye have shewed toward his name, in that ye have ministered to the saints, and do minister. (Hebrews 6:10)

To the **"family"** of Impact Church, you're the greatest. Your commitment to the vision in your prayers, attendance, ministry of helps and giving is unparalleled. I have preached around the world and there is no place like **"home."** Even other ministry gifts that speak at Impact acknowledge the hunger and pull they sense as they deliver God's word. None of this would be possible without you. You are highly favored of the Lord.

And once again, to our personal executive assistant, Sonya (So) Pinckney, for your "labor of love" in believing in the God in us. You make me laugh when I need to, your honesty and forthrightness is what makes you who you are. Thank you for knowing "who I am" and "how I am" and still working with me. Your work on this manuscript was such a blessing. Pastor Leesa and I love you greatly.

Clarification

Prophet Tim Hines and I want to make it clear that we are not dogmatic on the exact calendar time frame for this 3rd Day. In the western world, we use what is called the "Gregorian" calendar which differs from the "Jewish" calendar. According to our calendar, January 1, 2001 began our new millennium, or what we are referring to as our 3rd Day. However, the Jewish calendar differs several years from ours. We are not trying to cause more rifts in the Body of Christ, but to simply acknowledge whichever calendar you use and/or refer to, we are at least in the first fruits of this awesome day. We are not scholars, just two called men of God with a message for the church that burns within our hearts. Please allow the message in these following pages to minister to you as they already have to us and others.

His servants
Apostle Don Hughes
Prophet Tim Hines

Introduction
Apostle Don Hughes

January 2001 was a pivotal year for the Body of Christ and ultimately the world. It began the 7th day since Adam and **the "3rd Day"** since Christ. Have you ever read this scripture?

But, beloved, be not ignorant of this one thing, that one day [is] with the Lord as a thousand years , and a thousand years as one day. (2 Peter 3:8)

This will be the greatest season the church has ever known. Revelation and spiritual insight is increasing at a pace rivaling modern technology. It seems as if what has been proclaimed, preached and prophesied for the last several decades is unconditionally true, God has reserved the **"best"** for last. Keep in mind these truths are new to us, not Him. The church is growing up, we are putting away childish things, and we are coming out of process prepared for His glory.

Recently the Holy Spirit began to pull back the veil of revelation to me concerning the term, **"3rd Day"** throughout scriptures. Along the same time a true covenant friend of mine, Dr. (Prophet) Tim Hines began to receive incredible insight into the same subject. As we began to share with each other the truths God was revealing, the Holy Spirit arrested the both of us to put these truths into print. What you are about to read is something that has been God-breathed into our spirits. These truths will be released through an **"apostolic"** and **"prophetic"** mantle. Those who have ears to hear "**and receive**" will follow the cloud, others, as church history always proves, will stand still and proclaim they have "all truth" and aren't moving. If technology is progressive and we know it is, then so is revelation. The more "Lot" is removed from our lives (**see Genesis 13:14**) and when "Uzziah" finally dies (**see Isaiah 6:1**) we will see our destiny, our Lord and His revelation.

This book is our attempt to put **"into print"** what He has **"branded in our hearts."**

His servant by choice,

Apostle Hughes
Impact Church
Charlotte, North Carolina

Introduction
Dr. (Prophet) Tim Hines

I am very excited about sharing with you something that I feel and believe will shake heaven and earth. The Spirit of wisdom and revelation is a powerful down payment given to every believer from the Lord. The Lord said to me at the first of the year (2004), "Do not be afraid to discern people and times with My word." I feel that the church is at a cross road, there are those who are content with where they are and with what they have, and then there are those who are hungry for more of what God has to offer. In the following chapters, we will see how the Spirit of revelation will keep us on the cutting edge of what God will do in the earth. It will keep us open to the counsel of God's Word and how to be pliable to a fresh boulevard of ministry that will help us reach our generation. Many of us have lost our desire to reach out to others because we have lost our passion to be reached by Him in a deeper and more intimate way. It is the move of God in our life that moves us to achieve His mission. Passion plays a very important part in our relationship with the Lord. Not to sound critical, but our passion is the missing ingredient in most of the churches in America today.

We will see that revelation is the path that God travels to bring us into His present day truth. I have learned that we cannot be found in the operation of new truths if we have and old approach to things. Any type of new truth must have with it, a practical plan of application, it's called, **wisdom**. If it doesn't, it is useless. Wisdom shows us how to apply truth to our lives. It shows us how to do what God would do if He were in our situation. The Spirit of revelation has and presently will engraft to our souls salvation that will save us a fresh. The order of leadership is changing, God is moving in new directions and we must change and move with Him. It has been the Spirit of revelation that has brought us to the place that the church is presently at and it will be the Spirit of revelation that will take us to newer and greater heights concerning where we are headed.

Let this book stir your heart to maximize your relationship and your calling in Him.

Your servant in His service
Dr. Tim Hines
Tim Hines Ministries
Beverly Hills, Florida

Contents
From The "3rd Day"

Dedication:	*Apostle Don Hughes*
	Prophet Tim Hines
Acknowledgements:	*Apostle Don Hughes*
Clarification	*Apostle Don Hughes*
	Prophet Tim Hines
Introduction:	*Apostle Don Hughes*
	Prophet Tim Hines

Chapters 1-6 by Apostle Don Hughes
Chapters 7-12 by Dr. (Prophet) Tim Hines

Chapter 1
Apostle Don Hughes
Preparation For The "3rd Day"

Prophetically and strategically we have entered the greatest "day" (season) that the church and ultimately the world have ever seen. Do you remember this verse?

To every [thing there is] a season, and a time to every purpose under the heaven: (Ecclesiastes 3:1)

The church is now in a "set time" pre-ordained by Father God Himself. It is a season for **impartation, revelation and manifestation**. He is imparting revelation through his "gifts" like never before preparing His church and the world for "His appearing." We have entered the season where the manifestation of His glory will be seen wherever revelation is flowing. The church has become lethargic and complacent with endless (man-made) programs and services that produce nothing more than a temporary fix. We continue to prophecy to the "external" that which we can see, yet the "internal" (the cause of the external) goes untouched and even unnoticed. This is all changing, **the "3rd Day"** is here, we have begun to walk in unparalleled revelation, and Holy Ghost manifestations are increasing. Pure moves of God (not man structured) are upon us. Are you in position? Are you ready? I see a cloud the size of a man's hand (**1 Kings 18:44**).

Y2K

The clock was moving, second after second towards midnight, leaving 1999 and stepping into January 1, 2000. Supposedly the next great catastrophe according to all the modern day doom and gloom prophets. One little computer cliché was going to bring mass chaos to the world. Again ignorant (un-discerning) people (many of them Christians) were buying up every generator, flashlight and battery they could find. They were buying astronaut food and cleaning off the shelves of grocery and hardware stores preparing for another pending disaster. They had no problem spending money and even going in debt to try and "be ready" for what was "inevitable" according to the media. Several weeks prior to that evening, I was praying concerning how the church was reacting to all the ongoing hype as we moved closer to that day. The Holy Spirit spoke so strongly to me and said, **"Son Y2K simply means YES 2 THE KINGDOM. The new millennium will cause many to turn back to me who have been duped by the delusion of the world and even religion. Manifestations of my glory and revelation will increase."** Last time I checked, that day came and went without incident. **WHY? Because it was a declaration of "their day" not "HIS." This "3rd Day" is about HIM, not us! It is a revealing of HIM, not more religion. It is about us decreasing and HIM increasing!**

A Little History

Let's start with a little history. In the gospel of John, **Chapter One**, we see Jesus being baptized in the river Jordan. John proclaims Him as, "the lamb of God that taketh away the sin of the world." (**John 1:29**) He comes out of baptism to be immediately led into the wilderness (by the Spirit...see **Matthew 4:1**) to be processed (tempted). He comes out of his process having passed the test then he begins to call to the destiny of men. He "calls" his disciples. Watch this! Baptism, Process, Disciples...all preparation for what? *The "3rd Day"*! In **John 1:51** (the last verse of **Chapter One**) it states:

And he saith unto him, Verily, verily, I say unto you, Hereafter ye shall see heaven open, and the angels of God ascending and descending upon the Son of man.

Look at the prophetic declaration! Jesus declares that heaven is about to open and God's messengers will be "rising up and walking" (the definition of ascending and descending from the Greek language) in their position in Christ. And then, the first verse of **Chapter Two** starts with, "And *the 3rd Day*..."

There Was A Marriage

And *the "3rd Day"* there was a marriage in Cana of Galilee; and the mother of Jesus was there: (John 2:1)

As we stated in the "introduction" **(2 Peter 3:8)** declares that **"one day is with the Lord as a thousand years, and a thousand years as one day."** If you understand prophetically God's "days," we are in the seventh day from Adam and *the "3rd Day"* since Christ.   God exhorts us to not be "ignorant" of His "days."   Notice what one of the Old Testament prophets declared concerning this "day" that is upon us.

Come, and let us return unto the LORD: for he hath torn, and he will heal us; he hath smitten, and he will bind us up. After two days will he revive us: in *the 3rd Day* he will raise us up, and we shall live in his sight. Then shall we know, [if] we follow on to know the LORD: his going forth is prepared as the morning; and he shall come unto us as the rain, as the latter [and] former rain unto the earth. (Hosea 6:1-3)

Did you notice that at the end of "two days" we return to the Lord? We are the ones who have gone astray, we have left Him. Lost sheep, prodigal sons and daughters are "coming to themselves" and returning home. The Lord is healing, repairing and restoring us.   He is "binding" us, putting us back together.   At the end of the second day (or 2000 years) he began to "revive" (revival) us. Remember, "revival" is for the church, "evangelism" is for the world.   It has been hard to reach the world with a church that has needed the physician. Towards the end of the year 2000 (the 2nd day) outbreaks of revival spread throughout the world.   Hosea's prophetic insight was coming to pass...but WAIT!

- 4 -

"After two days will he revive us: in *the 3rd Day* he will raise us up..." (Hosea 6:2a)

God promised to "raise us up" in *the 3rd Day*. He is raising up those who have fallen, He is raising up those who have grown weary in well-doing, He is raising up those that the church and society have written off, He is raising up a valley of dry bones that will become an exceeding great army and they will do great exploits for Him. The term "raise us up" is the Hebrew word "quwm" (koom) which translates, "to establish, to confirm." It also comes from another word meaning "that which comes upon, causing to stand up, to band together, to excite a riotous gathering of people." In this **"3rd Day"** God is establishing His people; we are coming together and standing up once again. The joy of our salvation is being restored; zeal is coming back "to" and "for" the house of God. **GET READY!** There is a "riot" coming!

Father God is raising us up to **"...live in his sight" (verse 2b)**. I love how this translates. God is raising up a people who live in His presence, a people who is before His face, a people who have His countenance. Glory to God! Notice **verse 3** starts with the word, "then" which is referring to *the "3rd Day"*. We will know (be intimate with) Him and His manifestations. His presence in *the "3rd Day"* is referred to as "rain." Watch this! The word "rain" (Hebrew—"yarah" yaw-raw) in **verse 3** interprets like this, "those who teach, archers that shoot, those who inform and instruct, those who throw water." Can you see it? In *the "3rd Day"* God is revealing HIS revelation through His gifts, those who teach, instruct, inform, shoot (straight) and throw water (word). Do you remember this scripture?

I have planted, Apollos watered; but God gave the increase. So then neither is he that planteth any thing, neither he that watereth; but God that giveth the increase. Now he that planteth and he that watereth are one: and every man shall receive his own reward according to his own labour. (1 Corinthians 3:6-8)

In the last part of **Hosea 6:3**, the prophet states that the manifestation of the Lord will be as the "former & latter" rain. The former rain of the past has **"produced"** the crops **BUT** the latter rain is designed to **"mature"** the crops. This latter rain is "growing us up" and preparing us for His glory. It is time to come into His fullness; it is time to put away childish things. The kingdom of God is at hand! I stand amazed, after almost three decades of ministry, at those in the body of Christ who still want to hold on to **"their"** hurts, wounds, issues and immaturity when God is speaking to the "higher calling" within us. May the blinders be removed to whatever is hindering our destiny. Deep is calling to deep **(Psalms 42:7)**. Are we listening? Are we anticipating the supernatural intervention of God in this day? It is time the church become more like the image of the one they are "made in"! Let me give you another "prophetic" point to consider. In **Luke 10**, Jesus is teaching on what we often refer to as the story of the "good Samaritan." The good Samaritan ministers to the wounded man then takes him to an "inn" (this word comes from two Greek words which translate as "a public meeting place for everyone where they are brought into the family and embraced, taught and educated"). **Sounds like the church to me! Now watch this!**

And on the morrow when he departed, he took out two pence, and gave [them] to the host, and said unto him, Take care of him; and whatsoever thou spendest more, when I come again, I will repay thee. (Luke 10:35)

The good Samaritan gave the "host" two pence. A pence was a "days" wages. A "day" with the Lord is as what? "...as a thousand years, and a thousand years as one day." The word "host" defines as "an inn keeper who instructs, trains, and educates." I believe the application here is two-fold:

1. **The inn keeper is a reference to the Holy Spirit who is the teacher.**

2. **The inn keeper is also a reference to the shepherd, the pastor who is anointed, called and used by the Holy Spirit to help heal, restore and educate those who have been wounded and left for dead.**

The Samaritan (Jesus) stated that His appearing would be after "two days" or 2000 years. He would reveal (appear, manifest) Himself in *the 3rd Day*.

Watch what Nehemiah's enemies began to declare as he started re-building the wall.

But it came to pass, that when Sanballat heard that we builded the wall, he was wroth, and took great indignation, and mocked the Jews. And he spake before his brethren and the army of Samaria, and said, What do these feeble Jews? will they fortify themselves? will they sacrifice? will they make an end in a day? will they revive the stones out of the heaps of the rubbish which are burned? (Nehemiah 4:1-2)

The enemy will begin to declare out of fear and mock you when you are moving into your miraculous God destined day. Look what Sanballat says, "will they make an end in a day?" In other words, "The wall and gates had been torn down so long; do they really think there is any hope of rebuilding or any means of restoration available?" He proceeds to ask the question, can stones be revived, and can stones which have been burned and cast aside be used again? Of course, **the answer is yes**! In this day, God is reviving His stones (us) that have been overlooked, cast aside, left for dead, He is using those who have been burned (those who have gone through the fire). Did you know that a stone (brick) that has been "fired" is stronger than in its original state? **God uses burnt bricks! I love to declare it like this: GOD IS RAISING THE REMNANT OUT OF THE RUBBLE TO BRING A REVIVAL!**

We have entered *the "3rd Day"* or the 3rd 1000 years since Christ. Did you know that the meaning of the numeric number 1000 is "Divine completeness and the Glory of God"? The first day (1000 years) man was coming into the understanding that the unity he had had with sin and darkness had been broken. It was his "independence day" his day of deliverance, freedom and liberty. The second day (1000 years) man has been learning of his union with Christ. It has been a season of becoming a true witness and receiving revelation. The first two days (2000 years) all happened preparing us for *the 3rd Day*. This new day, this new millennium is taking us on to perfection, it is about resurrection power, and it is about **HIS MIGHTY ACTS**. This is the day God will **"show up and show off."** We have moved from the "outer court" first day to the "holy place" second day and are now going beyond the veil into the "holy of holies" "**3rd Day**." The first day was all about man (outer court), the second day was all about God and man (holy place), and this new **"3rd Day"** is all about **GOD** (holy of holies).

Chapter 2

And The 3rd Day There Was A Marriage

And *the 3rd Day* there was a marriage in Cana of Galilee; and the mother of Jesus was there: (John 2:1)

What was taking place on *the "3rd Day"*? A marriage ceremony was in progress, a covenant was in the process of being established. But wait! Something or SOMEONE was missing. This ceremony had just concluded its second day and as they began *the "3rd Day,"* it was brought to their attention that the wine had run out. The marriage was taking place in Cana of Galilee.

Cana was not only the place of Jesus first recorded miracle, it was a village known for an excellent spring of water. This spring rose up within the center of the village and flowed into the Mediterranean Sea. On the way to the sea it flowed past Ephraim to the south and Manasseh to the north.

Galilee is interesting in the Greek language. One of the Greek words is #63 "agrauleo" (ag-row-leh-o) and translates "to live in the fields, to be under an open sky (heaven), even at night."

Now let me put this together prophetically. In this **"3rd Day,"** we are coming into the understanding of the power of the Holy Spirit (river) that resides within us. It is designed to bubble up and flow (**see John 4:14**). Praying in the Spirit causes the river to flow. Everything we need "in Christ" is already "in us." Release the river, let it flow. As the river "in you" begins to flow, it flows past Ephraim and Manasseh. Ephraim means "double fruit" and Manasseh means "causing to forget." There is a flow or revelation and manifestation coming in this **"3rd Day"** that will bring about great fruit and great blessing. I heard one minister say once, "double for your trouble." To "flow" in this **"3rd Day,"** you must "forget" (Manasseh) those things that are behind (**see Philippians 3:13**), you must release the hurts and wounds of the past, you must forgive and forget. You can do this through prayer in the Spirit. All this will lead to a "Galilee" experience, "the opening of the heavens, even in your darkest hour."

And both Jesus was called, and his disciples, to the marriage. (John 2:2)

Did you notice that Jesus **and** his disciples were "called" to this event. They did not just show up! We have been having church our way for years and have seen little compared to what the scriptures promise us. WHY? We have been doing our own religious thing (because religion knows how to go through the motions of so-called church) whether God shows up or not. We can sing, shout, testify, give and not even realize that no one ask HIM to come.

Jesus **and** His disciples were called in ***the*** ***"3rd Day."*** There is a remnant of God's people hungry for truth, they are thirsty for fresh water. The day of "hiring" (which becomes a hireling) some preacher who won't rock the boat, one who will tickle the ears of lethargic, complacent, comfortable saints is over. There are some "disciples" (Greek "mathetes" math-ay-tes), men and women of God who have been learning at the feet of Jesus, they have been hidden on the back side of the desert, they have been called, processed and prepared for this **"3rd Day."** They have increased in knowledge and have an understanding of the "day" we are in.

And when they wanted wine, the mother of Jesus saith unto him, They have no wine. (John 2:3)

In the beginning of ***the "3rd Day,"*** they found themselves in want. What they had produced out of their own ability and consumed wasn't enough, they still were not fulfilled. **Verse 3** says, "when they wanted wine." The word "wanted" is the Greek word "hustereo" (hoos-ter-eh-o) which translates "to lack, to come up short, to fall short of the end, to be inferior in power, influence and rank, to be left behind in the race so you fail to reach your goal." What were they in "want" of? **WINE!** One translation says, "when the wine failed." Much of the church worlds programs, religious ideas, and plans have left them in want, still thirsty, and unfulfilled. We have been settling for a **"cheap imitation"** instead of pursuing the original. God forgive us! Today you can get imitation Channel, Gucci, Rolex, etc., because people don't want to pay the price for the original, the workmanship in the original is what makes it valuable. The materials they use are far more superior than those which produce a copy. For the last "two days," or 2000 years, we have run the gamut of "man made" programs and ideas, for the most part temporary in their results. People have become disinterested in "religious" church; they have experienced discouragement and disappointment at the results we have produced through our own ability. We have been found in "want." **For many, church is no longer a priority! Don't quit, *the 3rd Day* is here - truly the best is before us.**

The Making Of Wine

In ancient days the making of wine had tremendous prophetic insight for us today. They would take ripe fruit, place it into a vat and begin the "treading" process. The treading was done by one or more men depending upon the size of the vat. During the treading process they would encourage each other by "shouts." The juice produced from the treading process would stain their bodies and garments. Once the juice was expressed from the fruit, it was then taken and placed into what they called "vessels." They would then take the vessel that contained the juice and bury it in the earth so the fermenting process could begin. It was kept in the earth until wine was produced and then be removed for a special occasion. The longer it remained earthed, the stronger the wine and its aroma became. The longer it was "hidden" (aged) the more valuable it turned out to be. With this in mind, look at this scripture:

But we have this treasure in earthen vessels, that the excellency of the power may be of God, and not of us. (2 Corinthians 4:7)

The word "treasure" (Greek-"thesaurus" thay-sow-ros) translates as "a storehouse, a place where valuables are kept, where precious things are collected." Now let me break this down to how this affects us today. Many of us have produced some degree of fruit and thought that was the most important thing. We have been impressed with fruit, God wants it turned into wine. When you find yourself in the middle of the "treading" process, look around you, there are many in their "vat" in the same process and they need a shout of encouragement just like you do. Encourage one another, no one necessarily enjoys the "vat" process but they will the outcome. There are things within the church "individually" and "corporately" that have been aging for the last "two days" (2000 years). It is valuable and precious and has been hidden in an "earthen vessel." It is the excellency of God's power within us. He is releasing HIMSELF through us to a world desperately in need of the "original", not another counterfeit. God has been filling up His vessels with water (The Word) for the last "two days." It has entered us as "water" it will exit us as "wine." As I am writing this book, the Holy Spirit just reminded me of a scripture that now takes on new meaning.

Be patient therefore, brethren, unto the coming of the Lord. Behold, the husbandman waiteth for the precious fruit of the earth, and hath long patience for it, until he receive the early and latter rain. (James 5:7)

This is my paraphrase of this verse:

Fellow believers, don't lose heart while waiting for the Lord's presence to be revealed. The vine dresser is looking for the fruit he paid a great price for to show up in his earthen vessel becoming wine. He is patient because he knows that the early rain "produces" the fruit and the latter rain "matures" the fruit. (Apostle Hughes paraphrase)

The Lord has been very patient allowing the rain to work in our lives. WHY? **First to produce the fruit, then to mature the fruit, then to process the fruit into wine!**

Do you remember the Apostle Peter's statements to the people concerning what took place in **Acts 2**?

But Peter, standing up with the eleven, lifted up his voice, and said unto them, Ye men of Judaea, and all [ye] that dwell at Jerusalem, be this known unto you, and hearken to my words: For these are not drunken, as ye suppose, seeing it is [but] the 3rd hour of the day. But this is that which was spoken by the prophet Joel; And it shall come to pass in the

last days, saith God, I will pour out of my Spirit upon all flesh: and your sons and your daughters shall prophesy, and your young men shall see visions, and your old men shall dream dreams: And on my servants and on my handmaidens I will pour out in those days of my Spirit; and they shall prophesy: And I will shew wonders in heaven above, and signs in the earth beneath; blood, and fire, and vapour of smoke: The sun shall be turned into darkness, and the moon into blood, before that great and notable day of the Lord come: And it shall come to pass, [that] whosoever shall call on the name of the Lord shall be saved (Acts 2:14-21).

The Apostle speaks to the people who are seeing this awesome manifestation and says, "These folks are not intoxicated the way your mind perceives them to be." In other words, "it's not what you think, this is something new." He went on to say that it was only the **"3rd hour"** of the day, 9:00 am. The Jews seldom ate at this hour during their festivals and they always took their drink at meal time. Just another thought to consider, the #9 represents "finality, gifts, fruit (nine gifts of the Spirit, nine fruit of the Spirit) but also **birth** (a woman carries for nine months). In this **"3rd Day,"** we are giving birth to something that can't be compared with anything else. Manifestations are coming at the "3rd hour" of the day, a time when people aren't expecting these kinds of manifestations. God is preparing us for harvest. The fall season of God is upon us, the grapes have been gathered, the wine presses are working, And WINE IS COMING! By the way, the feasts are divided into **three seasons**. The last season is referred to as the "feast of in-gatherings."

Chapter 3

Preparing for the Miracle

Jesus saith unto her, Woman, what have I to do with thee? mine hour is not yet come. (John 2:4)

Jesus wasn't being disrespectful to His mother. It actually refers to God's timing. He was waiting until the exhausted supply of "their" wine was realized by all, then there could be no doubt as to the magnitude and the origin of the miracle. He has been allowing us for "two days" to do our "own thing" and calling it "**HIM.**" Our man centered ideas have run out, all of our **"how to"** seminars and conferences have left us unfulfilled and disillusioned. Many are beginning to call for Jesus and His true disciples to come to our gatherings.

Servants Requested

In **verse 5** the order is established prior to the miracle. Many of God's people and much of His house have forgotten that He is a God of order.

His mother saith unto the servants, Whatsoever he saith unto you, do [it]. (John 2:5)

There must be obedience from the servants (Greek "diakonos" dee-ak-on-os) deacons, there must be the heart of a servant evident in us in this day.

There must be obedience by those serving and those in leadership. In this story they were out of "wine" not water. It might have seemed foolish to those present to do what Jesus mother had said. Her words were powerful! **WHATSOEVER HE SAITH...DO IT!** Remember God has chosen "foolish things" to confound (put to shame) the wise of the world (**see 1 Corinthians 1:27a**). How many times have we questioned the things we knew God was speaking to us to do? How many times have we said, "that can't be God" knowing full well in our hearts it was?

Six Water Pots

And there were set there six waterpots of stone, after the manner of the purifying of the Jews, containing two or three firkins apiece. (John 2:6)

The water pots were there because of the cleansing rituals of the Jews. They were sticklers for washing, before meals, after meals, after traveling, etc. There were "6" water pots of stone. Six is the number of man in the Bible. We have been in a season of great emphasis being placed on the **Word of God (water)**. Why? Because the water level (word) in the church has been low. It has been diluted and misrepresented to the point in many churches that it is no longer the **"center"** of the service. God knew to bring about the magnitude of this **"3rd Day"** manifestation that there needed to be an increase in the water (word) level of his stone pots. Remember what cleanses us:

- 19 -

That he might sanctify and cleanse it with the washing of water by the word, That he might present it to himself a glorious church, not having spot, or wrinkle, or any such thing; but that it should be holy and without blemish. (Ephesians 5:26-27)

It isn't the **"vessel"** that cleanses, it is what is **"in"** the vessel. It still amazes me as to how much religion's emphasis is on the "exterior" of the vessel and so little on the "interior." Jesus hit the religious structure of his day head-on and rebuked them sternly for this mind set.

[Thou] blind Pharisee, *cleanse first* that [which is] *within* the cup and platter, that *the outside* of them may be clean also. Woe unto you, scribes and Pharisees, hypocrites! for ye are like unto whited sepulchres, which indeed appear beautiful outward, but are within full of dead [men's] bones, and of all uncleanness. Even so ye also outwardly appear righteous unto men, but within ye are full of hypocrisy and iniquity. (Matthew 23:26-28 italic emphasis added)

The Word (Water) Movement

Jesus saith unto them, Fill the waterpots with water. And they filled them up to the brim. (John 2:7)

Jesus directs the servants to fill the water pots with water. I thought it was interesting that the

- 20 -

marriage party asks for "wine" and Jesus called for "water." Today many within the church are asking where the wine (manifestation) is and Jesus is asking "where is the water" (word). WATER (Word) is necessary to produce WINE (manifestations). The word "fill" is the Greek word "gemizo" (ghem-id-zo) which means to "fill full to the point of overflowing." For the last 30+ years (the closing of the 2nd day) there has been great emphasis on the importance of God's word. People know it by different names (The Word Movement, Word of Faith, Faith Movement, etc.), but ultimately it has been a revealing of who we are "IN CHRIST." The water (word) level has been rising; the Holy Spirit has been preparing the church to release the "best wine" in this **"3rd Day."** The water pots "vessels" have been filled and are now being released throughout the world.

Draw Out NOW!

And he saith unto them, Draw out now, and bear unto the governor of the feast. And they bare [it]. (John 2:8)

The "governor of the feast" was basically the superintendent of the dining room. The word "governor" is the Greek word "architriklinos" (pronounced—ar-khee-tree-klee-nos) which translates as "the table master, the ruler of the feast." He was the one who placed the furniture in order, arranged the tables, and the food and also the order in which it would be served. He also tasted the food and wine before it was served. Who does this represent today? The 5-fold ministry gifts that prepare and taste the meals prior to the congregation (through study and prayer), arrange the order of the service and in what order the food (word) will be served. A closer look at the word "governor" conveys even greater prophetic insight. WATCH THIS! (I hear Bishop Eddie Longs voice in my mind). Governor also translates from a compound of two other Greek words as "a dinner bed composed of **three (3)** couches." The governor served a meal in three courses. As you finished each course, you would move to the next couch (room) and partake of the next portion of the meal.

God's pattern exists of three (3) rooms. Outer court...Holy Place...Most Holy Place! His desire is to feed us with the **"...sincere milk of the word..." (1 Peter 2:2)** that we may **"grow up into him in all things..." (Ephesians 4:15).** In the outer court (1st room), you become **"sin conscious"**, in the Holy

Place (2nd room) you become **"self conscious"** and in the Holy of Holies (3rd room) you become **"God conscious."** The first day from Christ (1000 years) produced an understanding of who we are **"without"** Christ. The second day from Christ (1000 years) produced an understanding of who we are **"in"** Christ. **The "3rd Day"** from Christ (1000 years of which we have just begun) is producing the revelation of who we are **"as"** Christ (in the earth). I know! I hear people gasping for breath right now! I am pushing the envelope; I am trying to get the church to think outside the box of stale, lethargic religion. The word **"Christ"** is the Greek word **"Christos"** (khris-tos, Thayer's #5547, 5548, 5530, 5495) which translates as "the anointing, to furnish with necessary powers for administration, to endue Christians with the gifts of the Holy Spirit, to handle and make use of God's might, activity and power." The Apostle Paul announced to the church at Corinth that Christ has a "many membered body" in the earth. His "christos" has "diversities of gifts, differences of administrations, and is diverse in his operations." He gives different manifestations of his "christos" to different members of His body. For example: word of wisdom, word of knowledge, faith, healing, miracles, prophecy, etc. He has many expressions of himself through his many membered body which makes up the church. Remember the mystery that was hidden from generations, but NOW is made manifest, "Christ **IN** you, the hope of glory" (**see Colossians 1:26-27**). Can you **SEE** it now?

The Holy Spirit is drawing out **NOW** what has been maturing (aging) in us and releasing it to a parched (waterless) church and world. Don't worry!

There are many governors (ministers) that are about to have their theology messed with. When they finally taste what heaven is **NOW** producing and stop serving up and eating what the last generation "canned", there will be great repentance, restoration, and refreshing in God's Kingdom. OH YES...The Glory will cover the earth (**Habakkuk 2:14**).

The Water That Was Made Wine

When the ruler of the feast had tasted the water that was made wine, and knew not whence it was: (but the servants who drew the water knew;) the governor of the feast called the bridegroom, (John 2:9)

The manifestation of this **"3rd Day"** will not be perceived by "observation" but by "participation." The Bible says "when the ruler of the feast had **tasted**" (Greek "geuomai" ghyoo-om-ahee) translates as "perceived the flavor of by partaking and enjoying." When men and women of God begin to partake of what is being released, when we as ambassadors of Christ begin to prophesy: **"O taste and see that the Lord is good..."** (**Psalms 34:8**), those who have settled for "a copy," those who have settled for "man made" will experience the real, the original, the best, that has been reserved for the last.

The Good Wine Until NOW

And saith unto him, Every man at the beginning doth set forth good wine; and when men have well drunk, then that which is worse: [but]

thou hast kept the good wine until now. (John 2:10)

Look at this verse in light of where the church has been. How many times has a minister "tried out" (by the way which is completely unscriptural) to be voted into some church. He/she will come with their best "stem winder" to get "hired" then when they become a "hireling" they just go through the motions preaching warmed over 2nd day messages over and over simply "changing" the title to protect the innocent. God forgive us! We have so intoxicated the church with our "lukewarm imitation" leftovers (yesterdays meal "message" that has been refrigerated "gotten so cold" that it has to be re-heated) that most in the body haven't perceived that there "IS" a difference.

The words "well drunk" is the Greek word "methuo" (meth-oo-o) which is defined as "to become drunk or intoxicated." We have duped the church into believing that what we have been "experiencing" is IT! We have it all! There isn't anything else. Our revelation is **the "ONLY"** and it is **the "TRUTH."** When you are intoxicated, your senses are not keen, your vision becomes impaired, and your reaction time to danger is effected. We have been drinking man made "cheap wine" and calling it the "best." It is going to take something "never tasted" to awaken the church out of its drunken stupor and come to our senses. I prophesy to you that God's best is NOW being released; the church is ready for a true **"3rd Day"** wine tasting" party. We have been singing "ain't no party like a Holy Ghost party" but haven't seen the manifestation yet. God is once again reversing the order and releasing **"HIS best"** at the last. In **(John 2:10)**, the Greek word for "now" is "arti" (ar-tee) which defines as "held in suspension until this NOW moment, time, or season. The time has come and NOW is when God is releasing His "water turned wine" out from His church and into the world. There is a "Holy Ghost" wake up call, we are coming to our senses and realizing that we have settled for much less than God's best. Get ready...the cork has popped and this **"3rd Day"** outpouring is **HERE**!

In closing this chapter, let's look at Hosea, the prophet.

I will heal their backsliding, I will love them freely: for mine anger is turned away from him. I will be as the dew unto Israel: he shall grow as the lily, and cast forth his roots as Lebanon. His branches shall spread, and his beauty shall be as the olive tree, and his smell as Lebanon. They that dwell under his shadow shall return; they shall revive [as] the corn, and grow as the vine: the scent thereof [shall be] as the wine of Lebanon. (Hosea 14:4-7)

The true churches backsliding state has come to an end. Worship has come back to His house; once again the rain is falling, and His people are growing. **Zechariah 14:17** declared when the people of God would not worship, God would send NO rain. They are returning to proper authority and covering (under the shadow). There is a "reviving" and "growing" taking place. The words in **verse 7** "revive as the corn" speak of "increase and multiplying" and "grow as the vine" deals with "prosperity." And finally His restored, worshipping, growing church is producing the "scent" of the wine of Lebanon. Lebanon translates as "whiteness" which is a reference to purity and also means "being brought to the point of your destination." The church will fulfill its "destiny" and reach her "destination."

Chapter 4

A 2nd Day Mindset

The greatest critics of any new move of God (new to man...not to God) are those who proclaim (through their own ignorance) that they already "have all revelation." I have been studying and preaching God's word for 30 years (as of January 2005) and have come to the realization that I don't know much. The more revelation I receive, the more I realize how little I know. What we call "moves of God" are really **seasons in God's plan** where He emphasizes certain "logos" (written truths) which become "rhemas" (revealed truths). Usually in these seasons, "gifts" are emphasized as well as "truths." Example: In the 1940's and 50's, it was healing crusades emphasizing the healing and miraculous power of God generally through "healing evangelist" (notice, "truths and gifts"). The Charismatic season followed with a fresh emphasis on being "filled with the Spirit" and the Body of Christ at large was operating in the "gifts of the Spirit." Next came the season where the emphasis was placed on the importance of God's word (the WORD movement). We were learning who we were "In Christ" and the importance of making God's word first place in our lives. We learned how to apply God's word in every situation we faced. The "teacher" and "pastor" were used mightily in this season (again notice "truths" and "gifts"). Somewhere sandwiched in these seasons the truths of "prayer & intercession" came forth as well as "prosperity," again the "teacher" was greatly used.

Shortly after came an emphasis on "prophets" and the "prophetic." Prophets were rising up, seers in the Body of Christ declaring the word of the Lord. Churches began flowing in prophetic worship and dance, songs of the Lord flowed, there were prophetic conferences being held around the world. And NOW the season of the "apostles" and the "apostolic" is upon us. Apostles are setting things in order that the "prophets" have seen and declared. Apostolic conferences and meetings are on-going world-wide and the church is being put back in order. Biblical government is being restored to the church, both individual and corporate. Governmental "truths" are being restored and established through "apostolic" ministry. (For an in depth study of why we have produced an impotent church, order my tape series, "Government Before Glory").

Now herein lies the problem. We have made "monuments" out of "movements" (seasons). Then we built museums (excuse me...churches) to house our old artifacts and relics (Thesaurus: leftovers, ruins, residue, remainder, what's left). We have believed a lie that says you have to "leave behind what you have learned" to "move **forward** and operate in a new season." What ever happened to the scriptures we all preach but then don't **do**? Moving from "faith to faith" and "glory to glory"? This is a deception spawned from hell itself and released through a religious cemented (set, hardened, and can't be moved) mindset. We have become the very thing we have preached about. Do you remember this?

And unto the angel of the church of the Laodiceans write; These things saith the Amen, the faithful and true witness, the beginning of the creation of God; I know thy works, that thou art neither cold nor hot: I would thou wert cold or hot. So then because thou art lukewarm, and neither cold nor hot, I will spue thee out of my mouth. Because thou sayest, I am rich, and increased with goods, and have need of nothing; and knowest not that thou art wretched, and miserable, and poor, and blind, and naked: I counsel thee to buy of me gold tried in the fire, that thou mayest be rich; and white raiment, that thou mayest be clothed, and [that] the shame of thy nakedness do not appear; and anoint thine eyes with eyesalve, that thou mayest see. As many as I love, I rebuke and chasten: be zealous therefore, and repent. (Revelation 3:14-19)

We think because we have stayed in a "past season" and built a memorial to it, that God is pleased with us. It is not important how "we see" us, it is important how God "sees us." We have said things like "we have arrived, we have all truth, we are SELF (not God) sufficient, and we don't need anything else." But God is saying something different. Look at my paraphrase of **verse 17** from the Greek language:

"Because you say *(I didn't)* that you are abounding in material resources and Christian virtues, because you say *(I didn't)* that you are affluent in resources so you can give blessings (but you don't) and because you say *(I didn't)* that you have need of nothing or no one, you cannot perceive or discern that you are only enduring toils and troubles *(not overcoming them)*, you are miserable *(unhappy, afflicted, brokenhearted, depressed, discontented, downcast, hurting, and wounded)*. In reality you are reduced to a beggar, you are destitute of influence, position, honor, wealth and Christian virtues; you have descended to a lower place. You have no mental perception because pride has put a smoke screen around you that you cannot see through and finally you lay naked and uncovered *(by your choices)*. *You are out of order!* **(Revelation 3:17)** (Apostle Hughes paraphrase, personal thoughts added in **bold *italics***)

Remember! This verse was written to a church that had become "lukewarm." We have allowed the same Laodicean (ruled by the people) mindset to come in our churches and we are NOW reaping the harvest of man-chosen leadership who are hirelings, thus afraid to speak the truth. We voted "impotency" into our pulpits and then wonder and even complain that our churches aren't producing. This "out of order" system is responsible for church splits, schisms, spiritual AIDS and adultery. We have ended up recycling sheep instead of birthing new ones. It is time for the apostles who are called, appointed and anointed by God to bring order back to God's house where **HIS** glory can fall.

How many more of God's people will die this side of the Jordan (**seeing...yet never possessing their destiny**) because of an old mindset?

We must allow the Holy Spirit to remove our Egypt (world) mindset; we must allow Him to reveal the religious pharisaical mindsets that so many operate through under the guidelines of "religion." God is moving; don't let an old "frame of mind" keep you from following him!

Over the next few chapters, let's look at a passage of scripture in depth that the Holy Spirit has opened to me prophetically concerning a 2nd Day "mindset." This 2nd day mindset is **the** major hindrance to receiving **"3rd Day"** revelation. Let's approach **Luke 24** with an "open mind" and see what the Holy Spirit has to say.

And, behold, two of them went that same day to a village called Emmaus, which was from Jerusalem [about] threescore furlongs. And they talked together of all these things which had happened. And it came to pass, that, while they communed [together] and reasoned, Jesus himself drew near, and went with them. But their eyes were holden that they should not know him. (Luke 24:13-16)

Let's update the events of this passage prior to **verse 13**. Mary Magdalene, Joanna, Mary (the mother of James) and other women approached the tomb on the first day of the week and found the stone rolled away. Two men in **shining garments** (will explain this later in the chapter) announced the resurrection of the Lord to those present. They returned and spoke those things to the apostles which again didn't believe (I too know what it means to share "3rd Day" revelation and see leadership and laity who refuse to move on also reject it). The Apostle Peter runs to the tomb to see for himself only to leave an empty tomb with internal wonderings.

Seeing But NOT Seeing

Cleopas and another disciple are headed to Emmaus...let's pick up the story here. In **verse 15**, the Bible says that **Jesus "came up along side of"** them and heard only a small portion of their conversation. Herein lies the problem which is two-fold. First, they didn't recognize him; secondly, they didn't recognize his voice. **Verse 16** states, **"...their eyes were held that they should not know him."** The word "eyes" is very revealing in the Greek language. It is the Greek word "ophthalmos" (of-thal-mos) which translates as "the eyes of the mind, the faculty of knowing." In other words, these two disciples **saw**, but they had no **perception** of who it was walking and speaking with them. **WHY? They were walking with a "3rd Day" revelation, still operating out of a 2nd day mindset!** Think about it! Jesus asks them the question in **verse 17**.

"What manner of communications are these that you have one to another, as ye walk, and are sad?"

Their conversation was producing sadness. The word "sad" is the Greek word "skuthropos" (skoo-thro-pos) which defines as "a sad countenance, a sad gloomy (depressing, dim, overcast, dark) countenance." It comes from a derivative meaning "to see, appear, to look." Their conversation was based on things they had **"seen"** not on things they **"knew."** They were talking about what Mary Magdalene and the other women had **seen**, they were talking about what Peter had **seen**. Look closely at **verse 11**:

And their words seemed to them as idle tales, and they believed them not.

Idle tales is the Greek word, "leros" (lay-ros) which means "idle talk, nonsense." Idle means "empty, inactive, immobile, inoperative." All too often the churches conversation is based on what things **appear to be** rather that what it **knows** (or should know). We **watch** the news; we **look** at the daily newspaper and make decisions accordingly. Have we forgotten this powerful verse?

While we look not at the things which are seen , but at the things which are not seen: for the things which are seen [are] temporal; but the things which are not seen [are] eternal. (2 Corinthians 4:18)

The Apostle Paul told the Corinthian church that the things that are seen (to behold, to perceive by the use of the eyes...natural) are temporal (endure only for a while, subject to change). Most of the hurtful things people hang on to and talk about are things that they **saw happen to others or themselves**. I know what it may **look** like in your life right now, however, change your focus, and shift your attention to what is eternal. **Eternity in you can change the temporal in front of you!**

Logos...RHEMA

In **(Luke 24:17)**, Jesus ask the two men, "...what manner of communications" were they speaking with each other? The word "communications" (are you ready for this) is the Greek word "logos" (log-os) which translates as "a word which embodies a conception or idea," or ultimately, "the written sayings of God." The problem with today's **impotent church** is that it has become so religious and fearful that all it cares about is protecting its past move "logos" (that which God emphasized in seasons or moves past). With every new season, with every fresh move comes a "NOW" word from God. A word (logos) that literally comes alive (rhema)! Now, it is not about what God **has said** but what **HE IS SAYING**! Present tense! Many main stream denominational churches today refuse to follow **present day truth** because they have spent decades preaching about what God **has said**. Anytime someone comes along and declares, prophesies, and preaches what **God is doing or what He is saying**, they are branded a heretic, false prophet, or worse. Maybe now we can understand how Jesus must have felt when he came to the earth. **He was the written (logos)...revealed (rhema)! He was the logos become rhema! He was the word made flesh! We need the rhema to tabernacle among us!**

In **verse 18**, Cleopas could only respond to Jesus question based on what **"had happened"** thus missing what was **"presently happening."** *The 3rd Day* revelation (rhema) was before him and he couldn't see Him/it because his thought pattern was stuck in the past. Be careful! An un-renewed mind can keep you in **"what was"** instead of following and flowing in **"what is."** **It isn't a devil causing you sadness...It is an old mindset.** Jesus continues asking in **verse 19, "And he said unto them, What things...?"** Look at the doubt-filled words of Cleopas, "...concerning Jesus of Nazareth, which **was** a prophet..." By the way, Jesus of Nazareth was not a revelation of who He **"was,"** it was information concerning where He **"was from."** We thought He was a prophet, we thought He was mighty in deed and word, we thought He was the redeemer of Israel (yada, yada, yada). The King James Bible uses the word "trusted" in **verse 19** which is an inaccurate translation. It is more often defined as "hope." Listen to these two statements and you will see the picture more clearly. #1) I trust you! #2) I **hope** I can trust you! They didn't **trust** that He was the one; they were "a hoping and a praying." Cleopas begins to close his discourse with these words:

But we trusted that it had been he which should have redeemed Israel: and beside all this, _today is the "3rd Day"_ since these things were done. (Luke 24:21)

This is *the "3rd Day"* and I am confused, this is *the "3rd Day"* and I have forgotten that He said He would rise again on this day, this is *the "3rd*

Day" and I am sad, this is **the "3rd Day"** and I am missing it because I am stuck in an old mindset, this is **the "3rd Day"** and...!

Chapter 5

TODAY is The "3rd Day"

As we continue with the same thought, let's go further into the revelation. Jesus finally responds to Cleopas' dissertation with a strong rebuke in **verses 25-26**.

Then he said unto them, O fools, and slow of heart to believe all that the prophets have spoken: Ought not Christ to have suffered these things, and to enter into his glory?

Jesus called them fools! Now if He would have said that to a typical church attendee today they would have responded with statements like, "I am out of this church, that isn't love, nobody is going to tell me the truth (excuse me,...talk to me) like that, and other excuses why they don't have to grow up." The word "fools" is interesting in the Greek. It is the word "anoetos" (an-o-ay-tos) which speaks of one "not understanding or perceiving with the mind." There are over 60 verses in the Bible dealing with the subject of "fools." How often have we been in an anointed prophetic service where a fresh prophetic word is being preached or prophesied and our old pattern keeps us from receiving present truth? Jesus rebukes them and says "you are slow of heart." What they were **"experiencing"** on *the "3rd Day"* had already been established by the mouth of the prophets. The **spoken** was being **revealed** and their mind set coupled with their conversation was causing them to miss the revelation (Jesus) that was right before them. The word "slow" is just as strong in the Greek. It is the word "bradus" (brad-ooce) which describes a mind that is inactive, slow to apprehend or believe and **stupid** (ouch). Jesus continues to tell them that Christ had to suffer all the things spoken of to reveal a glory (revelation) yet to be revealed. Their minds were still stuck on where Jesus was from (Nazareth), not who He was! Let's look at another passage of scripture briefly that ties in with this thought.

And Simon Peter answered and said, Thou art the Christ, the Son of the living God. And Jesus answered and said unto him, Blessed art thou, Simon Barjona: for flesh and blood hath not revealed [it] unto thee, but my Father which is in heaven. And I say also unto thee, That thou art Peter, and upon this rock I will build my church; and the gates of hell shall not prevail against it. And I will give unto thee the keys of the kingdom of heaven: and whatsoever thou shalt bind on earth shall be bound in heaven: and whatsoever thou shalt loose on earth shall be loosed in heaven. (Matthew 16:16-19)

Peter didn't respond to Jesus question by saying **"you are the Nazareth"** he said **"you are the CHRIST."** You are the revelation, the manifestation, of that which has been spoken. The Apostle also uses the word "living" in reference to Christ. Fresh revelation is not wrapped in the old religious structures echoing nothing more than yesterday's manna. It is alive, living, fresh, strong and full of life (see the Greek word "zao" for the word "living"). **It is NOW!!!** Jesus expounds further by saying to Peter "...flesh and blood hath not revealed it unto thee..." There are a lot of "flesh and blood" doctrines (those given by religion) that bring no **KINGDOM REVELATION!** Look at another verse that shares even more insight.

And this gospel of the kingdom shall be preached in all the world for a witness unto all nations; and then shall the end come. (Matthew 24:14)

Jesus didn't say the gospel according to man, religion, or public opinion. Paul, the Apostle stated the gospel is the "power of God" unto salvation (**see Romans 1:16**). It is the power to perform miracles, it is the power and influence which come from riches and wealth, it is inherent power manifest, and it is miraculous (see the Greek word for "power" **dunamis**). The gospel of the kingdom is a gospel unmixed with the watered down message of man and his religious ideas. It is a pure gospel free from the "traditions of men" that make the word of God of none effect. Did you notice that this gospel is supposed to be preached to the whole world as a **"witness?"** In its simplest definition, the word **"witness"** can be translated as **"someone or something with evidence."** Christ **"in us"** wants to operate **"through us"** and all the church can think about is **"leaving"** (just a thought). Where is the evidence to what man has preached according to religion and its mindsets? The evidence that I see is a weak, bored, complacent, riding the fence of compromise people. It is an evidence littered with ministers who have grown weary and quit, it is an evidence of church splits, schisms, and finally thousands of churches no longer in existence. It is an evidence of untold amounts of sheep scattered, battered, beaten and left for dead while religion continued to walk by only to look on in disgust. It is an evidence of these same sheep jumping from sheepfold (church) to sheepfold hoping this one will heal them from their wounds and bleeding. The problem is that the **"pulpit"** in these places is bleeding as much as the **"pews."** I think you see my heart. There is a **"kingdom gospel"** in this **"3rd Day"** that is a word with "revelation, impartation and manifestation." It is healing the hurting, challenging and changing the complacent. It is reforming wrong religious mindsets and causing us to think **"outside"** the box (by the way...which God has been "out of" for a long time).

This dangerous mindset has caused the religious community to pack its **"get out of here"** bags, sit down on its **"blessed assurance"** *and do nothing!* Yes, the Lord is coming back to His church, but if His own disciples missed the signs even where His resurrection was concerned, how much more are we missing the signs...thus not found doing? Do you remember this part of the verse in **(Luke 18:8)**?

"...Nevertheless when the Son of man cometh, shall he find *faith* on the earth?" (*Italics* is my own emphasis)

Now herein lies the problem, if we don't **"believe"** (have faith), we sure won't be **"doing."** **Faith without corresponding action is dead!** Peter, the Apostle, missed a sign concerning the resurrection of the Lord. Mary Magdalene and the other women had returned from the tomb and shared with those present what they had seen. Peter then runs to the sepulcher to see for himself. Let's look at **(Luke 24:12)**.

Then arose Peter, and ran unto the sepulchre; and stooping down, he beheld the *linen clothes laid by themselves*, and departed, wondering in himself at that which was come to pass.

John's gospel reveals another aspect of what Peter missed.

Then cometh Simon Peter following him, and went into the sepulchre, and seeth the linen clothes lie, And the napkin, that was about his head, not lying with the linen clothes, but *wrapped together in a place by itself.* (John 20:6-7)

The **"napkin"** was the cloth used to cover the head of the corpse. This was separate from the linen clothes that wrapped the body. There was a tradition (known among those in Jesus day) that when an individual left a table and was only leaving for a "season" they would fold their napkin and leave it at their place at the table. This signified to all that **"saw"** the folded napkin that the person who had left was only gone **"temporarily."** It was a **"sign"** of their eminent return. When Peter ran into the tomb, he found the sepulcher **"empty of a body"** but **"present with a sign"** yet his mindset caused him to miss the sign.

Are we so busy, so "wrong prioritized," that we are missing the signs of our season of visitation, revelation and impartation?   The prophet Amos declared that the Lord would reveal His secrets (**His day**) to and through His prophets (many don't even believe in this gift). If we have been listening to the prophets...we should KNOW what God is doing.

Surely the Lord GOD will do nothing, but he revealeth his secret unto his servants the prophets. (Amos 3:7)

Have we lost the joy of our salvation, have we lost our zeal for God, has our intimacy been affected because of familiarity? The greatest day (*the "3rd Day"*) is upon us, Christ is being revealed in a manner like never before, revelation is increasing, and manifestations are multiplying. **Today** is the day of salvation!

Chapter 6

Messengers of The "3rd Day"

As we proceed into the last chapter of my part of this book, let him that hath an ear, HEAR what the Spirit is saying to the church **(Revelation 2:7)**. For a moment, let's go back to the beginning of the story in **(Luke 24)**.

Now upon the first [day] of the week, very early in the morning, they came unto the sepulchre, bringing the spices which they had prepared, and certain [others] with them. And they found the stone rolled away from the sepulchre. And they entered in, and found not the body of the Lord Jesus. And it came to pass, as they were much perplexed thereabout, behold, two men stood by them in shining garments: (Luke 24:1-4)

The Bible states that there were **"two men"** standing before them in **"shining garments."** They saw two men on **the "3rd Day"** that didn't look like any they had seen during the **2nd day**. Before the religious Sanhedrin stone me, hear me out! The word for **"men"** is the Greek word "aner" (an-ayr) which comes from another primary word "anthropos" (anth-ro-pos) which translates as "man, male, a man-faced human being." It also translates as "to distinguish man from other beings, animals, God, or even angels." Briefly let's look at a synopsis (comparison) of the four Gospels regarding this story:

Matthew 28:2	**"One angel sat on the stone"**
Mark 16:5	**"A young man sitting"**
Luke 24:4	**"Two men standing"**
John 20:12	**"Two angels"**

The word for **"angel"** is the Greek word "aggelos" (ang-el-os). At times it does define as **"angel"** but not that alone. It also means "one who is sent, a messenger, one who brings tidings, an envoy (a representative, a diplomat, an ambassador), or a messenger from God." Now let me give you another thought to consider. In **(Revelations 2-3)**, John reveals what Jesus spoke concerning the seven churches. He begins His exhortation to each church with the statement "unto/and to the angel of the church of." Yes, the word for "angel" is the same Greek word "aggelos" (as stated above) to all of the seven churches. But here is the problem! **ANGELS DON'T LEAD CHURCHES...PASTORS DO!!!** As I looked at the word even further, this prophetic truth came forward. The word "aggelos" is derived from the word "ago" which means to "bring forth, to lead" which also comes from the word "agele" which translates as a "herd or company." Can you see the prophetic insight? It is the pastor who is **a** (there are other gifts that are God's messengers also) messenger for God, bringing forth and leading a company into the destiny and plan of God for their lives. Let me impart something to you that the Holy Spirit revealed to me as I first began to study the material for this book. Look closely at Mark's gospel concerning the story of the resurrection.

And when the Sabbath was past, Mary Magdalene, and Mary the [mother] of James, and Salome, had bought sweet spices, that they might come and anoint him. And very early in the morning the first [day] of the week, they came unto the sepulchre at the rising of the sun. And they said among themselves, Who shall roll away the stone from the door of the sepulchre? (Mark 16:1-3)

We will explore two key words in **verse 3** that carry powerful prophetic insight concerning these **"3rd Day"** messengers. The word **"stone"** is the Greek word "lithos" (lee-thos) which translates as "a stumbling stone, a stumbling block, an obstacle in the way which causes one to stumble or fall." The other word **"door"** is the Greek word "thura" (thoo-rah) which describes "an entrance which sheep go in and out of" it also translates as the "door of the kingdom." Can you see it? Who or what will remove the stumbling blocks or stones (people, ministers, religions, denominations) that are hindering the sheep from moving through the door of the kingdom. It is the **manifestation of CHRIST** in this **"3rd Day"** that will reveal and remove every obstacle that has kept God's people from seeing, hearing and doing. It is the **revelation revealed** through His servants in this **"3rd Day"** that will also demonstrate the **reality of redemption**. God has and is raising up men and women in this **"3rd Day"** that are not concerned with the "status quo" of religion. When God called me to Charlotte, North Carolina, he spoke this to me "I didn't call you to this region to be "popular" but "powerful." When God's messengers begin to share things that are new (once again...not new to Him), religious sparks always fly, when its not religious rhetoric that everyone is familiar with, the words "false, new age, cult," etc., generally follow. Church history is full of men and women that received insight/revelation then refused to back down when religious leaders threatened to "Excommunicate" them. Those truths outlived their religious counterparts. Truth will always prevail! Back in **(Luke 24:4)** it describes the two men wearing "shining garments." It could read that these two men shined externally because of the light internally. Revelation on the **"inside"** will bring manifestation to the **"outside."** Do you remember what happened to Moses on Mt. Sinai?

And it came to pass, when Moses came down from mount Sinai with the two tables of testimony in Moses' hand, when he came down from the mount, that Moses wist not that the skin of his face shone while he talked with him. And when Aaron and all the children of Israel saw Moses, behold, the skin of his face shone; and they were afraid to come nigh him. And Moses called unto them; and Aaron and all the rulers of the congregation returned unto him: and Moses talked with them. And afterward all the children of Israel came nigh: and he gave them in commandment all that the LORD had spoken with him in Mount Sinai. And [till] Moses had done speaking with them, he put a vail on his face. But when Moses went in before the LORD to speak with him, he took the vail

off, until he came out. And he came out, and spake unto the children of Israel [that] which he was commanded. And the children of Israel saw the face of Moses, that the skin of Moses' face shone: and Moses put the vail upon his face again, until he went in to speak with him. (Exodus 34:29-35)

Moses in a **"higher place"** was having a visitation and impartation with the God of Glory! The rest of the people in a **"lower place"** were doing their own thing, playing church, living a lifestyle of complacency and compromise. Moses received more than the **"ten commandments"** during that encounter with God. In the Hebrew, when it says, **"...the skin of his face shone..."** it literally states that his face **"sent out rays."** The impartation (revelation) received on that mountain was so powerful, what he encountered in the face of God exploded out of him. The people at the bottom of the mountain were not used to someone exhibiting that kind of manifestation except for **God Himself**. Moses was speaking such incredible things to them that rays of light were coming out of his being. They weren't ready for that kind of truth, so the revelation had to be veiled. I am not trying to be crude here but I must give this analogy, when a man is veiled (covered) during intimacy, the seed of life stays with him, it never enters the womb, thus no conception. Let me prophesy right here:

*The veil has been removed, true intimacy is available, and the seed of **revelation received** will produce a **harvest of manifestation**. God desires "face to* *face" with His people. Men and women of God, unveil the revelation God has given and is giving you and release it into your family, church, region, state and the world. The greatest manifestations are NOW to be revealed, be delivered from the face of man and stay in the face of God, the fruit that will come forth in this* **"3rd Day"** *will not be denied!*

Another point of interest to me is the meaning of the word "Mt. Sinai." It defines as "the place of thorns." It is out of those **pierced difficult places** that true revelation comes forth. Let's look at these verses in **(Luke 24:27-28)**.

And beginning at Moses and all the prophets, he expounded unto them in all the scriptures the things concerning himself. And they drew nigh unto the village, whither they went: and he made as though he would have gone further.

Jesus begins to expound beginning with whom? Moses, then the prophets. Who/what was He revealing on that road that day? **Verse 26** states He was speaking of **CHRIST!** If the prophets wrote in scripture concerning Christ, and they did, then why did He include Moses and begin with his name, unless Christ was revealed to Moses on that mountain also. The Bible says that He acted as if He were going to continue walking and leave them. Why? I believe that He was testing them, He was checking to see how hungry and open they were to the things being revealed. Notice what **verse 29** states:

But they constrained him, saying, Abide with us: for it is toward evening, and the day is far spent. And he went in to tarry with them.

Jesus was preparing to walk away when **verse 29** says that the men **"constrained"** Him. The Greek language demonstrates the strength of this word. It is the Greek word "parabiazomai" (par-ab-ee-ad-zom-ahee) which defines as "to compel by employing force." Christ was being revealed right before them, their mind set was changing, and revelation was manifesting. They were not going to miss their "day of impartation." Oh, that the church of today would become that hungry for present day truth, that we would perceive revelation when it is being revealed and not turn loose. They convinced Jesus (by their actions...remember, actions speak louder than words) to come into their house. In **verse 30**, He takes them further.

And it came to pass, as he sat at meat with them, he took bread, and blessed [it], and brake, and gave to them. (Luke 24:30)

Notice, as they sat down to eat, He took the bread (which can also be translated as "shewbread") and blessed it then broke it before He gave it to them. When you break something open, what is on the inside comes into view. One of the definitions for the word "shewbread" is "the purpose is the setting forth of a thing, placing it or bringing it into view." Example: When God opened Adam, Eve was revealed, when the Roman soldier opened up the side of the last Adam (Jesus), the church was revealed. **When**

we are opened up, Christ is revealed! I know in my own life, during seasons of brokenness, revelation came forth that amazed me. I personally believe that the greatest revelation comes out of brokenness. Truthfully, we don't really know what we believe **UNTIL** what we believe is tested. **Verse 31** is so powerful:

And their eyes were opened, and they knew him; and he vanished out of their sight.

The word **"eyes"** here is the same Greek word used in **verse 16**. It translates as "the eyes of the mind, the faculty of knowing." In **verse 16** these same men could not perceive the revelation that was in their midst because of a 2nd day mentality. Now Christ was revealed, the revelation of *the "3rd Day"* was manifest. Their minds were "opened" Greek word "dianoigo" (dee-an-oy-go) which defines as "to open by drawing asunder, to open thoroughly what had been closed, **a male opening the womb (*the closed matrix*)**. Jesus (the word) was opening the womb of these men's hearts to receive **"3rd Day"** truth. He was depositing the incorruptible seed within them. The dictionary defines the word "matrix" as "something **within** which something else originates or develops." Once our spiritual womb is open to present day truth "...and they knew him..." (**Verse 31**) conception happens. The Greek word for "knew" is "epiginosko" (ep-ig-in-oce-ko) which translates as "to become **thoroughly** acquainted with, to know **accurately**." It also derives from another word meaning **"position"**, and finally, it is a primary verb the Jewish people used for **"sexual intercourse."**

We must position ourselves to receive this intimate truth that is being revealed. Do you want to know **about** Christ or do you want to know Him **thoroughly/accurately**? There are ministers around the world that are not fearful of declaring the truth that Christ is revealing in this **"3rd Day."** Our church has positioned itself to receive what God IS DOING in the earth RIGHT NOW!

One final thought for you to consider at the close of these writings. The last part of **verse 31 states "he vanished out of their sight."** The word "he" is a reference to Jesus. Usually we will capitalize an "h" when it is in reference to Him. The translators used a lower case "h." The **CHRIST** had been revealed, planted in their womb (matrix), Jesus the man was gone. Look at this verse of scripture:

To whom God would make known what [is] the riches of the glory of this mystery among the Gentiles; which is *Christ in you*, the hope of glory: (Colossians 1:27 italics added for emphasis)

The greatest season of revelation and impartation is upon us. My prayer is the truths revealed in this book will challenge you to pursue the presence of God. Present day truth is being unveiled by many of God's gifts! Follow the cloud, don't settle for complacency. Don't settle for the good or acceptable; don't settle for 30 or 60 fold, don't settle for outer court/holy place. The Spirit of revelation is upon us, don't miss this impartation!

Chapter 7
Prophet Tim Hines
Are you Hungry for a "3rd Day" Word?

In those days, the multitude being very great and having nothing to eat, Jesus called His disciples to Him and said to them, "I have compassion on the multitude, because they have now continued with me "three days" and have nothing to eat." "And if I send them away hungry to their own houses, they will faint on the way; for some of them have come from afar." (Mark 8:1-3)

The Apostle Mark opens this chapter by saying; **"In those days."** We live in a time where most of the church world seems to just be existing. The lack of passion and pursuit for more of the Kingdom seems normal with the present day believer. People today only want to give a part of their lives to His call and service and not all of their lives. I know and feel that the season for God is beginning to change again. To be found in position for where we are going, it will require a completely committed heart. We must understand that the God we serve is a moving God. In **Genesis Chapter 1**, we see Him moving on the face of the deep, and in **Revelation Chapter 22**, we see Him a soon and coming King. From the beginning of the Book to the end, we see Him moving. The challenge is **"can we flow and move ahead with Him?"** To simply say yes, could be too easy. We might not know now what will be required of us, but I do feel that this next move of God will require one thing, and one thing alone, *Faithfulness.*

Faithfulness to whatever the Lord is requiring is not always simple. It means we must be open, pliable, and willing to see things differently. For example, the Lord said to me that the year 2004 would be the year of promotion or a year of revisiting the old problems. He went on to share with me, that this year was an open door year. But, He said that there was a quandary at hand, He went on to say, **"My people are too big to go through the door."** I asked Him what this meant, and He said **"its pride and religion that will keep people from following me to another level."** Let me show you how the Spirit of revelation can challenge our present day walk. If you were to do a study on the Tabernacle of Moses, you would find that there are three doors that lead to three different areas. Each door can be measured to be found at one hundred cubits each. One hundred in the Bible refers to, *"The election of grace."* We can not come into the Body of Christ without a born again experience. If we were to add the second door with the first doors measurements, you would have the number, two hundred. Two hundred in the bible means *"Insufficient.'* If we are not careful, we can take being referred to as insufficient, as a bad confession. Something that is outside of who I am in Christ, but, in reality, it is impossible for anyone of us who are in Christ to move ahead through that 3rd door without the Spirit of Revelation leading the way. Revelation is something that no one can make happen. ***We must*** *simply siege opportunity in the life time of the opportunity.* It is God who opens doors that no one can open, and it is God who shuts doors that no one can shut. I feel to walk successfully with the Lord; we must realize that we are insufficient to walk in revelation, no matter how much we know or how long we have served Him. All we have to do to be successful in any timing of the Lord is to just be faithful. Revelation will challenge where we are and show us that there is more. Joshua tells the Jewish people to take **three days**, to sanctify themselves before they cross over into the promise land. He says that the Lord will do wonders on that **"3rd Day."** I believe that we are in a **"3rd Day"** preparation. Why? Leadership is changing. If you'll notice that the people are no longer being lead by the cloud and over shadowed by the pillar of fire. The Ark of the Covenant has not been placed upon the shoulders of the priest and they are two thousand cubits out in front of the people. The Ark of the Covenant represents the presence of God, and we will talk more about His presence later. But, it is very evident that Leadership is changing. We will either follow the presence of God that will take us into many infallible proofs as we seek after His passion, or we will stay where men say we should stay, in the present. We must remember that the journey from Egypt to Canaan was only eleven days. Eleven is the number for disorder, and the number twelve is the number for Government. God was simply trying to get the disorder of Egypt out of His people so they could once again be established in His government for their lives. I think that we are at the same confrontation in time. They that are lead by the Spirit of God are the sons of

God. In today's church, this reality is becoming more and more, scarce. I assure you of this truth that the move of God will grow popular again. The origin of creation can be satisfied with one thing alone and this one thing is the presence of God. God never intended to give Israel a land, His real intensions were to give Israel Himself. The Spirit of Revelation in **the "3rd Day,"** I feel, will follow this same pattern. I'm talking about manifestations of Him in ways that only He and He alone, receives all the glory.

Jesus saw a great multitude that had nothing to eat. It is the Rhema of the Word of God that the Lord uses to open our hearts to embrace more of eternity. There are people in today's church that don't even take notes of the sermons that are being preached. We don't sit on the edge of our seats expecting and anticipating the move of God in our services. We don't even like services that last longer than one hour. Something is drastically wrong. The hunger and the passion of the past is just that, a thing of the past. The Spirit of Revelation will change everything. It will stir us to believe, it will prepare us for what is and what is on the way. It opens our souls to heal, prosper, grow and mature. Revelation will keep us from being halted between two opinions; it will make you a cut above those who have come to discover they no longer understand you. It will cause you to sail through what others have chosen to drown in. It will make you the outcasts of popular inner circles, but the celebrated one of God's inner circle. Revelation will cause you to walk, talk, think and act in faith. You'll no longer talk about the mountain, you'll talk to it. When others say, "You have missed the mark, you're off course, or you're out of your mind," revelation will call and cause you to rebuke the storms of life. Paul the Apostle wrote,

"That the God of our Lord Jesus Christ, the Father of Glory, may give to you the spirit of wisdom and revelation in the knowledge of Him, the eye's of your understanding being enlightened; that you may know what is the hope of His calling, what are the riches of the glory of His inheritance in the saints."

I want you to see that wisdom and revelation run hand in hand.

"Christ has been made unto you wisdom." (I Corinthians 1)

"If any one of you lacks wisdom, let him ask of God, who gives to all liberally and without reproach, and it will be given." (James 1:5)

(Job 11:6), says, That He would show you the secrets of wisdom. For they would double your prudence.

The word *"prudence"* here means strategy. If you thought that God's battle plans have worked for your good in the past, get ready for a double portion. God's wisdom is remarkable. Watch it work in prayer alone. There will be times that the wisdom of God does not allow our minds to be fruitful. While we pray, have you even wondered what you might have been praying in tongues while you were praying in the Spirit? *It is the Lords wisdom not allowing us to understand everything that we might be praying at the time that we are praying.* When we pray in tongues, or in the Spirit, we pray according to the perfect will of God. The Holy Spirit knows that we might not be ready to know all the facts that we are praying, as we pray them. It is God's system of wisdom that brings our souls into season, when He knows that we are ready to understand what God the Father already knows about us. It is the Holy Spirit in us that knows things about us that we are still yet to discover. It could be that if we were to understand what we pray, while we pray, that it might catch us a little off guard. We might look at what we are praying and say, "God, are you sure you're talking about me?" We all go through seasons of preparation. To know a certain Word or His Will, about yourself prematurely, could lead to doubt or unbelief. Because of a lack of ripeness and maturity, we might desire to stand in the way of His plans, instead of for them. God is too smart to make mistakes. We must trust our Father that He will make us ready when He knows we will be ready. It's the Spirit of Revelation that keeps us in agreement with the anointing. If we don't, revelation knowledge can't be revelation knowledge. Healing can't be healing, prosperity, deliverance, or breakthrough cannot be unto us what the Lord has intended it to be. The anointing destroys the yoke and undoes the burdens, stay in agreement with what the Lord is doing in your life.

Mark goes on to tell us that Jesus called His disciples to Himself. Any type of new beginning has a calling to it. I have watched Pastors and lay people talk about the next great move of God all across our nation. I want to share my heart with you when I say, that what is about to happen will either save to the uttermost, or separate those who do not want to go on to new and better things. There is a pattern found in the humanity of the church to get started with God only to be found located somewhere in the history of the church. In *(Judges 15:17)*, we see Samson throwing away a jaw bone of an ass that he has just used to kill one thousand Philistines with. The Spirit of Revelation is a timeless weapon given to the church to stay progressive with. God is no respecter of persons. What He will do for one, He will do for all. Each and every one of us has the same Holy Spirit within us, and He will keep all of us on schedule if we will allow Him to. Any new move of God is a calling but that calling is for all of the church.

Jesus told His disciples, **"I have compassion on the multitude, because they have now continued with me "three days" and have nothing to eat. And if I send them away hungry to their own houses, they will faint on the way; for some of them have come from afar."**

The word **"continued"** in the Thayer's commentary means, **they held fast to the grace of God that they knew were in the Gospels.** They knew like a remnant knows, that there is always more that the Kingdom wants to accomplish in our lives.

They were placing a **"3rd Day"** demand on Jesus. They were placing a demand on Him to bring forth something that would fill and complete them. ***They were hungry for the miraculous.*** Jesus said, that ***"He would not send them away hungry, for some of them have come from afar."*** I know people who have been in church for a long, long time, that have never really felt that they were a part of what was happening, people and churches that were not stuck in one revelation or one move of God. I'm not talking about people who kill anything new from heaven with strife because they have a spirit of control. I'm referring to people that did as the Lord told them to do, people that were people of character and of faithfulness. People who were willing to change and comply as the seasons of God brought freshness, people that have never seen the fruits of what the Lord has placed in their hearts to see. We know that 99.9% of personal prophecy is conditional. You can't expect to move into something fresh while remaining in yesterday's character. You can't put new wine into an old wine skin, but you can place water there. I'm not talking about people who want the water of yesterday's revelation. I'm talking about people who have done their best to stay on course with the cutting edge of the Lord, but have never really entered their season. One thing I can share with you that is a powerful truth, when He comes for you, when your season hits, it's supernatural.

(2 Thessalonians 1:10), *when He comes, in that day, to be glorified in His saints and to be admired among all those who believe, because our testimony among you was believed.*

(Acts 1:3) *says, to whom He also presented Himself alive <u>after His passion</u> by many infallible proofs, being seen by them during forty days and speaking of the things pertaining to the Kingdom.*

The "3rd Day" places us in alignment with predestinated plans that heaven wants to share with God's people. Hundreds of people are instructed to go to Jerusalem and wait for the out pouring of the Holy Spirit. When the Apostle Peter writes in **(I Peter 1:12)**, *To them, (referring to the old testament Prophets) it was revealed that, not to themselves, but to us they were ministering the things which now have been reported to you through those who have preached the Gospel to you by the Holy Spirit sent from heaven-things which angels desire to look into.*

This man knows what he is talking about. It was Peter who knew what the manifestation of God was when it hit in the upper room. It was Peter who said; *"For these are not drunk, as you suppose, since it is only the "3rd hour" of the day."* **(Acts 2:15)**

One translation says, *"That they were free to be their original selves."* They, through this manifestation of Heaven, had released them to find themselves and find the purpose of God for their lives like never before. This manifestation had no one's personality, no one's style or flavoring, but Gods. The Spirit of Revelation in this **"3rd Day"** season will do this very thing all over again. "Infallible proofs on the behalf of those who are after His passion, prophetic understanding of what the Lord is doing, and manifestations of His glory and grace that will save, deliver and heal." CHURCH! It's time to expect again. I know and believe that our best days are still in front of us. I feel that only a few things are required of us in this present hour, obedience to the personal assignments that the Lord has asked of us, faithfulness to our spiritual authority in our life, and expectancy. We must understand that the people could not partake of the miracle until they were willing to submit to the order that Jesus was requiring. Jesus' disciples were given instructions and then the people were given instructions for this feeding to manifest. I exhort you to stay on course, stay excited and ready to receive the next move of God.

Chapter 8

"Second Day Minds and 3rd Day Moves"

Therefore I also, after I heard of your faith in the Lord Jesus and your love for all the saints, do not cease to give thanks for you making mention of you in my prayers; that the God of our Lord Jesus Christ, the Father of glory, may give to you the spirit of <u>wisdom</u> and revelation in the knowledge of Him, the eyes of your (heart) understanding being enlightened; that you may know what is the hope of His calling, what are the riches of the glory of His inheritance in the saints. **(Ephesians 1: 15-18)**

As we enter a **3rd Day** age, the Holy Spirit will be there to open our hearts and minds to a deeper relationship with Him.   It is hard as a minister to reach guarded people.   People who have walls of hurt, and people that have walls of religion.   People that think that they have followed the Lord far enough, and think that they are as completed as they need to be. People do not want anymore information for personal change because it might inconvenience their lifestyle, but, God is able to reach all men, no matter where we are.   If we expect to dive into the deeper things of God, we must be a people who will pay the price for help.   Everything about allowing the Lord to heal and inform, produces thanksgiving.   ***The 3rd Day*** is arousing a desire, a passion for the moves of God again.   We know that we can not fight all of our battles with the Logos of the Word of God; we need a Rhema to win every battle. The fresh information through the wisdom of God is absolutely amazing. We know that in (**Galatians 1:12), Paul said; For I neither received it from man, nor was I taught it, but it came through revelation of Jesus Christ.** He went on to tell us in verse eighteen, **then after "*three years.*" I went up to Jerusalem to see Peter, and remained with Him Fifteen days.** The number fifteen means, "rest." Paul the Apostle is sharing with us that He was a very religious man before the Lord arrested His heart. After His conversion, the Spirit of Revelation took Him into the desert and spent "*three*" years revealing Jesus to Him. We now find Him spending "*fifteen*" days with Peter. I'm sure that most of this time; the Apostle Peter was bearing witness to all that the Lord had revealed to Paul. Paul after ***fourteen years*** returns to Jerusalem to share His heart with the leaders of the church once again. He has now tarried with the Spirit of Revelation another ***fourteen years***. This man was so very hungry for the things of God. This **"3rd Day"** age that we have arrived at brings with it, incite that will fill the hungry heart once again. Paul seems to be a little angry and disappointed with the Apostle Peter at this time. Peter was the one that the Lord Jesus Christ gave this **"3rd Day."** commission to. When Paul returns after spending fourteen (*fourteen being the number of deliverance and salvation*) years with the Spirit of Revelation, he sees, that he, himself, is under the same mantle that the Apostle Peter was under the last time they were together. He also sees the need to address Peter's conduct. Many ministers today fit this same pattern.

They don't have a problem getting started with a move of God, but it's letting that move prepare them for the next level.

The Spirit of Revelation prepares us for what is and what is on the way. It excites us, stirs us and fuels fresh passion. The Apostle John wrote in...

(Revelation 1:8)*, "I am the Alpha and the Omega, the beginning and the end." saith the Lord, "who was and who is to come, the almighty."*

We as believers can never be in a place that this timeless God hasn't been. And if He has been where we now are, then He has something to say about where we are now. I feel that the Spirit of Revelation is ready to open the heavens and bring us into more of eternity. We have a church today that for the most part is very fruitless. People are not interested in going to church, to prayer, or to the work in the ministry. But there is a remnant that has chosen to preserve through the many onslaught of humanist and the efforts of kingdom of darkness. A people who have been told the Holy Spirit's presence is not what will work in the Twenty-First Century. A people who have been told that to still believe in the power of God is old fashion. A people who have been looked down on because they hold fast to the Bible and it's convictions and not what seems to be popular by men. A people who dare to be misunderstood that somebody might see Jesus, people that have been accused of being off course, and out of their minds. Get ready remnant, to have the Spirit of Revelation and all that He has for us in the next move to appeal to the truth of who we really are and the reason why we have this unusual and unquenchable desire for more of God. Paul writes to a young Pastor by the name of Timothy. He shares with him in...

(II Timothy 3:16) that, All scripture is given by "inspiration" of God, and is profitable for doctrine, for reproof, for correction, for instruction in righteousness, that the man of God may be complete, thoroughly equipped for every good work.

If you thought that you were misunderstood in the past, get ready for the light to separate you even farther. Please see that inspiration concerning scripture first and foremost brings doctrine. The main doctrine of the Kingdom of God is *revelation*. God has always been and will always continue to be a moving God. The doctrines of the Word of God as they are engrafted to our souls are progressive acts of salvation. Revelation as we understand it is a progressive act of saving the soul. It is revelation that shows us the truth of reproof. Today, we have many people in the church who do not want to be confronted, and those who avoid any kinds of correction or instructions in righteousness. There are people who detest others who get too close to their issues with scriptural help, and those who want a feel good gospel that doesn't cost them anything. Holiness, tithing and God's order in the home is all a thing of the past. My friends, the anointing must be greater in your homes than it is in your church.

Otherwise, you will try and make your church look like your home. But Jesus said, in...

(John 7:17) "If anyone wills to do His will, he shall know concerning the doctrine, whether it is from God or whether I speak on my own authority."

Please remember that any move of the Spirit requires one thing, faithfulness.

There are many reasons why people will oppose a fresh move of God, but we will take time to explore four of these reasons. The first being the greatest:

1. ***We stop allowing the Word of God to reflect His destiny to our lives.*** In the gospel of ***(John 1:16)***, the Word of God proclaims, ***And of His fullness we have all received, and "grace for grace."*** The first word grace in this verse of scripture means, "Anti or oppose." And this last word grace means, *"The unmerited favor of God."* When we as believers stop allowing the spirit of revelation to show us precisely what God wants to show us about His Son, we end up opposing the unmerited favor of God. On the morning of the **"3rd Day,"** when Jesus was raised from the dead, Mary, the mother of Jesus, and Mary Magdalene brought this good news to Jesus' disciples. When both of these women saw Jesus alive, they wanted to touch Him, but He told both of them to not *"cling"* to Him. This word *"cling"* means to keep the same. When the disciples heard the news of the **"3rd Day,"** they had a second day

mindset that had at least to this point, kept Jesus the same. The report of His resurrection in *(Luke 24:11), says, And their words seemed to them like "idle tales" and they did not believe them.*

The word "idle" here means nonsense. There will be many who do not want to think or want to apply in their lives that they might need more of Jesus than what they have already. The move of God before it has started, has already been opposed with carnal logic. How many people do you know that think that the Gifts of the Spirit have been a thing of the past? In this next flow from heaven, we will see the glory of God that will draw men to repentance. From this present evangelism, will come the return of miracles to the church and the daily life of hungry believers. Normally, the ones that form such opinions are the ones that are idle in their relationship with Heaven. It can be just as easy for a believer who already knows the fullness of God to fall into the same trap. A believer who knows the presence and power of God, and has not been around or part of a move of God for awhile, this deception can linger. Jesus shares with us in *(Matthew 20:3), "And he went out about the "3rd hour" and saw others standing idle in the marketplace."*

Can I tell you as I travel from border to border of this great nation of ours, that, in most cases, there is little to no move of God? The church has become an idle identity. We have become a people of symbolism and we lack substance. The best thing that could ever happen to a church that fits this description is to lock the front door and burn the building to the ground before it is arrested for false advertisement. We have become a people where this seems to be ok. It's a trap that we will have to recover from, so that we can be anointed to finish the work that is at hand. I feel that in this **"3rd Day "**move of God, heaven wants to employ as many as are interested. Will you be part of the labors that Jesus will need to be sent into the harvest that is already ripe? Will you be bold enough to share in the persecutions of your Christ? **"Heaven wants to employ you!"**

2. *We claim ownership of a former move of God.*

In any season of God that brings with it revelation, there will also come a challenge, a confrontation by someone or something to see if we really believe what the Lord is sharing with us. The Word says in...

(Acts 23:12-13), And when it was day, some of the Jews banded together and bound themselves under an oath, saying that they would neither eat nor drink till they killed Paul. Now there were more than forty who had formed this conspiracy.

Paul's sister's son heard the discussion of the ambush and went and warned Paul about the Jews plan.

(Acts 23:23) says, And He called for two centurions, saying, "Prepare two hundred soldiers, seventy horsemen, and two hundred spearmen to go to Caesarea at the "3rd hour" of the night.

I have learned not to judge anything that I do not fully understand. Most Christians judge revelation and moves of God prematurely. When we do this, whether we realize it or not, we have put up a wall of defense. It could be that we end up not entering into the very thing that the Lord sent to save and deliver us in. Oddly enough that this planned attack against Paul's life took place at the *"3rd hour."*

I understand that there are those that will try and make revelation out of any little thing. But, let me ask you a few questions. How did you feel about the Charismatic renewal moment? the praise and worship movements? the intercessory prayer movement?   Or the joy movement that left everyone who entered into its outpouring laying and laughing on the ground?   How did you feel when you either heard or were around these types of services?   I have been apart of each of these outpourings.   They have enhanced and blessed my relationship with the Lord.   They have grown my walk with God in supernatural ways.   When each of these moves came into the earth, there were times that I didn't feel that I needed these manifestations in my life to walk in victory.   One thing we must always remember about manifestations in our life is to walk in victory.   One thing we must always remember about manifestations, it's not the experience that God is wanting, it's the fruit that is awakened in the heart of the believer from that experience that He is wanting. It is His desire for all of us to yield too and be apart of everything that He does in the earth.   Let's just be real here, its pride or embarrassment that keeps us from yielding to the Lord. When we pick and choose what we want to be a part of, then we find ourselves in jeopardy of claiming the rights of the movement. It's in this identification of a certain move or season that we define ourselves.   Instead of being on the forefront of what the Kingdom of God is doing, we have plateau and have become the defender of this movements rights. I know personally, so many people who just don't see the need for the move of God anymore in their walk. It's more of God that saves not only us, but others also because we chose to grow. It's more of God that makes us more effective and ready to be obedient whenever the Lord moves or calls.

(I Timothy 4:16) says, Take heed to yourself and to the doctrine. Continue in them, for in doing this, you will save both yourself and those who hear you.

This scripture alone places a burning desire in my heart to want to stay growing, maturing and fresh in the things of the Lord. People that are stuck in one movement, and can not see the need to move on in God, *are people who feel the need to be important.* In the last thing that the Lord has done is that they found a sense of achievement and identification of revelation that change the church, but it has become the last thing that the Lord did that is now keeping them from the next thing that the Lord wants to do. When this takes place, pride has a foot hold. **"God resists the proud, but gives grace to the humble."** It's pride and religion that keeps us from seeing that the Lord would have all of us to see and to stay fresh and prepared for the next level.

3. **We keep company with people who talk against those who think outside the box.**
People reproduce after who they are, not after what they say. Yes, *"out of the abundance of the heart, the mouth speaks."* Time and situations that are beyond our control will evidently find us out. Just because someone is talking the talk doesn't mean they are walking the walk. When we fail to capture the character of a revelation, we really do not understand or see what the Lord would have us enter into. We start forming an appearance of Godliness, but we lack the power thereof. When we really get serious about Holy Ghost power in our lives, revelation will be the key that opens our hearts. Spiritual ability is to do what needs to be done when it needs to be done. The Spirit of Revelation is a means to an end of our lives. Jesus did what He did at Calvary because He let the Father have His way. Progress in the Christian life is to surrender, conform and to become a greater servant. Can we be crucified like Jesus was and not stray from His nature? All that the Lord does in our lives at any season is to

make us all more like Him. Stay around people who have the same desire to know God like you do, and then let your light shine. Sometimes the best sermon preached is the life that we live. It's in abstinence that we discover who and where we are. Fruitlessness is designed to lead us to frustration. Frustration will push us to discover God in new ways or be content to stay where we are.

(Proverbs 26:7), tells us, Like the legs of the lame (A leg has become holt) that are not equal, Is a proverb in the mouth of fools.

Not everyone's walk will be the same. Just because someone around you chooses to limit their walk with God, it doesn't mean that you have to. Shoot high, stay hungry and go for the gold.

4. *When we find out how far we are really willing to go.*

(Genesis 22:1-4), Now it came to pass after these things that God tested Abraham, and said to him, "Abraham!" And he said, "Here am I." Then He said, "Take now your son, your only son Isaac, whom you love and go to the land of Moriah, and offer him there as a burnt offering on one of the mountains of which I shall tell you." So Abraham rose early in the morning and saddled his donkey, and took two of his young men with him, and Isaac his son; and he split the wood for the burnt offering, and arose and

went to the place of which God had told him. "Then on the 3rd Day, Abraham lifted his eyes and saw the place afar off."

It was at this time that Abraham was finding out how far he was willing to go. God knew the end from the beginning. Abraham needed to know the end result of his faith and trust in God's direction for his life. You don't have to be saved very long to find out that this Christian walk is designed to bring you and I to the end of our lives. We are in a time where our willingness to follow the Lord is showing the truth of our love for Him. On the *"3rd Day,"* Abraham saw where God wanted him to go and saw what the Lord wanted him to do, and he was willing to be obedient.

(Exodus 19:11), "And let them be ready for the "3rd Day." For on the "3rd Day", the Lord will come down upon Mount Sinai in the sight of all the people."

Moses was a man who was used to being in the presence of the Lord. He was a man that out of these times with the Lord, the people would have to cover his face because lighting bolts would be coming from it. Moses met with the Lord and God wrote on tablets of stone with His finger and gave him the Ten Commandments that would govern a people. In the presence of the Lord, what God placed in his hand, a staff became an instrument of deliverance and miracles. He was a man that spent forty days with God and the Lord showed him how to build a replica of the heavenly tabernacle in the earth. He loved the presence of the Lord, and God loved being with him. It has always been in the heart of God to be with His people, and have a people who wanted to be with Him. The Lord told Moses to tell the people to get ready to meet with Him on the **"3rd Day."** I want to tell you the same thing that Moses shared with the people in his time; we need to get ready to meet with the presence of the Lord. When the people came to the mountain where the Lord wanted to meet with them, the mountain shook because of the Lord's thundering and lightening. The people were frightened by the presence of the Lord. You would be surprised at how many people in the church today are afraid of the presence of the Lord. We should be a people that reverence His presence, but not a people that are afraid of His presence. We should never take for granted or become too familiar that we would disrespect the Lord's presence. But, in His presence, there is fullness of joy, unspeakable joy, holiness and purity beyond logic. In His presence, sin can not find a hiding place and our wills can not co-exist with His will. Any trace of rebellion instantly is made manifest only to leave us crying out for mercy. God is coming to meet with a **"3rd Day"** people, a people that want to be with Him as badly as He wants to be with them. The presence of the Lord, His glory, will be a main tool of evangelism in this next great move. We need to be a people that lift Him up at whatever cost, and we will see the power of our God.

(Hosea 6:1-3) says, Come, and let us return to the Lord; For He has torn, but He will heal us; He has stricken, but He will bind us up. After two days He will revive us; on the 3rd Day He will raise us up, that we may live in His sight.   Let us know, Let us pursue the knowledge of the Lord.   His going forth is established as the morning; He will come to us like the rain, like the latter and former rain to the earth.

We live in a time where the responsibility of bringing the Lord to people and the people to the Lord, rests upon the shoulders of a **"3rd Day,"** faithful remnant.

(Joshua 3:1-5), the Word says, Then Joshua rose early in the morning; and they sent out from Acacia Grove and came to the Jordan, he and all the children of Israel, and lodge there before they crossed over. So it was, after "three days," that the officers went through the camp; and they commanded the people; saying, "When you see the ark of the covenant of the Lord your God, and the priests, the Levites, bearing it, then you shall set out from "your place" and go after it. "Yet, there shall be" a space between you and it, about two thousand cubits by measure, Do not come near it, that you may know the way by which you must go, for you have not passed this way before." And Joshua said to the people, "Sanctify

yourselves, for tomorrow the Lord will do wonders among you."

This happens to be one of my favorite portions of scripture, because it reveals and dares to share the very nature of the Spirit of Revelation. After **'three days**" the **'officers**" this word means, *"An open door, used for an opportunity for something."* Men in leadership went throughout the camp telling the people that from that day forward, leadership was going to change. Colonials with the general's heart prepared the people to walk differently. Up to this point in time, they had been used to following a cloud, and this **'3rd Day**" was making things different. They commissioned the people, that when they saw things another way than the way they had seen it before, they were to go after it. Depending upon whose calendar you are looking at, the church is almost to the point prophetically in time where Israel had found herself. The Ark of the Covenant was placed upon the priest shoulders and carried two thousand cubits in front of the people. The Ark of the Covenant represented the presence of God, Gods glory and His power. And now, this change of order has found the priest to be the bearers of this responsibility. The church today has almost caught up with that two thousand year mark from Calvary to the present day. I feel in my heart that we are going to where only He has been. There is a crossing over into something very special. The presence, the power and His glory is coming upon the officers who are making ready a people for the coming of the Lord. As we study this story from **"the other side"** of the Jordan, *the promise land side,* we see many new beginning truths. The first thing that the Lord required of them was circumcision. Even though this was a physical act in the life of a Jew, it was really an act of the heart.

(Romans 2:28-29), says, For he is not a Jew who is one outwardly, nor is circumcision that which is outward in the flesh; but he is a Jew who is one inwardly; and circumcision is that of the heart, in the Spirit, not in the letter; who praise is not from men but from God.

In the life of a **"3rd Day"** person, circumcision of the heart is what we live for. Are we a people today that can still be instructed and taught new things in new ways? Are we a people who embrace reproof, correction and instruction in righteousness? If we can't, we are self destructing and we do not even know it. After circumcision was applied, the commander of the Lord's army came to meet with Joshua, and the first victory in this new season was won with a shout. I have already shared with you about the double portion of wisdom that is flowing with heaven filled strategy. Wisdom out dates the creation because it is in Him. But, I have always believed that miracles would return to God's people upon the wings of praise. The one thing that most church going people do not understand, is the one thing that will always work when nothing else will. When you can't pray, preach or prophesy your deliverance through, you can always praise it through. The commander of the armies of the Lord is giving a **"3rd Day"** *people* a new and illogical strategy that will produce heaven results. Are we really ready to meet with this commander of God's army? Are we ready to receive from this commander and chief, new walking orders? If we are circumcised in our hearts to love God with all of our heart, mind and soul and, if we are ready to release our faith, believe God and say to the mountain, be removed, I think that God is ready to fight this end time battle Himself.

"Behold, I send an Angel before you to keep you in the way and to bring you into <u>the place</u> which I have prepared. Beware of Him and obey His voice; do not provoke Him, for He will not pardon your transgressions; for My name is in Him. But if you indeed obey His voice and do all that I speak, then I will be an enemy to your enemies and an adversary to your adversaries. (Exodus 23:20-22)

We are finding our way to a **"3rd Day"** place in time. And God gives us the assurance that He will fight our battles for us. Why? When we are doing what the Lord would have us to do when He wants us to do it, we are invincible. Look at verses fourteen through nineteen. We see that God wanted His people to keep *three feast seasons.* Obedience belongs to us and the battle belongs to the Lord. Obedience has always been the foundation of our deliverance. All we have to do is be in the *place* (called time) where He would have us to be. We have been a self reliant people too long, getting what self reliant people can produce. It is time to return to the Lord and see what He wants us to do.

(2 Timothy 3:16-17), says, All scripture is given by inspiration of God, and is profitable for doctrine, for reproof, for correction, for instruction in righteousness, that the man of God may be complete, thoroughly equipped for every good work.

Notice that Paul tells us that the first thing that **"inspiration"** is for, is doctrine.   The main doctrine of the kingdom is that of revelation. God within Himself is Alpha and Omega, He was, He is, and He is to come. From the beginning of the Bible to the end, God is moving. Doctrine is the progressive acts of salvation. Not the immediate act of being born again, made alive by the Holy Ghost in our spiritually dead spirit man. It's the process, the act that saves our souls by the engrafting of God's Word. The Spirit of revelation is preparing a **"3rd Day"** people to be on the forefront of a fresh word and a fresh move of God, processed into this act of God that has been sent to save us.

Chapter 9

Three Crosses at the 3rd Hour

Then they compelled a certain man Simon a Cyrenian, the father of Alexander and Rufus, as he was coming out of the country and passing by, to bear His cross, And they brought Him to the place Golgotha, which is translated, Place of a Skull, Then they gave Him wine mingled with myrrh to drink, but He did not take it. And when they crucified Him, they divided His garments, casting lots for them to determine what every man should take, Now it was the "3rd hour," and they crucified Him. (Mark 15: 21-25)

At the cross of Calvary, we see a number of powerful truths that pertain to this **"3rd Day"** hour. At the cross, we see one dying **for** sin, one who dies **to** sin and one dying **in** sin. At the cross, we see a dying saint, a dying savior and a dying sinner. At the cross, we experience Christ on a cross, the world on a cross and a believer on a cross. Jesus at Calvary can save the unholy, the unfit and the unclean. At the cross, we see man at his worst, but God at His best. Christ and the cross will always be eternally nailed together. We as believers must see that Jesus did what He did at Calvary, because He chose to let the Father have His way. Jesus will never ask any man about the extent of his sin, but only about the reality of his desire to be freed from iniquity forever. If there is a place where man can be completely honest about the darkest areas of his life, it's at Calvary. The Apostle Paul said, **'We preach Christ crucified**." This is the only preaching that the Holy Ghost blesses and can use for the conviction of the sinner conscience.

"At the cross, at the cross where I first saw the light, and the burdens of my life rolled away, it was there by faith that I received my sight, and now I am happy all the day." (Hymn At the Cross)

Paul said, But God forbid that I should boast except on the cross of our Lord Jesus Christ, by whom the world has been crucified to me, and I to the world. (Galatians 6:14)

I feel in my heart that in this **'3rd Day** " call, the church is being challenged to live the realities of this revelation. For us to be completely successful in His call on our lives, we must live separately from the world. We are in this world, but we are no longer of it. Our main goal in life has become **"fulfilling His will."** Jesus said,

"My food is to do the will of Him who sent Me, and to finish His work." (John 4:34)

In the main portion of scripture shared with you at the opening of this chapter, we find a man being pulled from the crowd to carry the cross of Jesus. I feel a remnant people being pulled from a crowd to answer a new call, a picking up of a new mantle and a new anointing. A people who are coming into their God awakened character and their personal prophetic understanding. Calvary has always been the answer for man, and it will be at Calvary where the Holy Spirit shows this remnant people how to reach their generation. Simon might have thought that He was an innocent bystander that day, but the father had much more planned for him than that. Simon was later asked, "What was it like carrying the cross?" He replied, "when it was first placed on my shoulder, the weight of it almost knocked me to my knees. I gathered myself and began a journey that changed my life. I didn't understand where we were going and why this was happening, but all of my attention completely shifted when I felt something running down my neck, shoulder and arm. I looked to see what it was, and when I did, I saw that it was the blood of this man that I didn't know. Everything changed when I saw this man's blood, my attention was no longer on a yelling and violent crowd. It was no longer on the weight of this burden, in fact, His blood captivated me so, the cross was weightless."

"There is a fountain filled with blood, drawn from Emanuel's veins, and sinners plunge beneath that blood lose all their guilt and shame." (Hymn At the Cross)

When the devil sank his venomous fangs into the blood stream of humanity, it took someone coming in the likeness of humanity to redeem us. Jesus was and always will be the lamb slain from before the foundation of the world. He hung between heaven and hell in a hot Palestinian sun for you and me. He went to the depths of hell and took back the keys of death, hell and the grave for you and me. It was Jesus who was raised from the dead on this **"3rd Day "** that you and I would be free to live beyond the grave. When we see the blood spilt by this loving savior, truly the burdens of this life are rolled away. It was nothing but pure love that ran through His veins.

"What can wash away my sins, nothing but the blood of Jesus, what can make me whole again, nothing but the blood of Jesus, oh precious is the flow that makes me white as snow, no other fount I know, nothing but the blood of Jesus." (Hymn Nothing But The Blood of Jesus)

Simon was being chosen for a much bigger picture than what he might have realized on that day. Can I tell you today, you too, are being chosen for something that will always be bigger than you? This man's name, Simon in Hebrew mans, *"Shama. "* This word *"shama"* might not mean much to a western minded person, but to a Jew, it begins to speak volumes. When a priest stands up and speaks out the word *Shama*, one of two things had to follow. The reading of the Ten Commandments, or a proclamation that says this...

"Behold on Israel, the Lord our God is one God, He is Elahiem the creator of the heavens and the earth, the one who makes us holy through His covenant and His commandment."

This man Simon was a prophetic cry from our heavenly Father to a nation as he bore Jesus' cross that day, Simon, as he drug this cross through the streets, with every step, cried out, *"Behold oh Israel"* ...Simon of course had no idea what the Lord had chosen him for. His very name speaks to a nation that still can not see who He was and who He is. But, as he carried the cross, His name spoke loudly, *"Behold oh Israel, the lamb slain before the foundation of the world, He is one God. (there He is) our God, He is Eliahiem. He will make us holy today."* Simon I'm sure, did not know what the Gentile people have come to know. He did not see himself the way a born again child of God can now see himself. But, it is and it was evident that he was chosen to prophetically point the way to the future. The nation of Israel did not see or hear his prophetic call as he himself paraded before a nation that yelled **'crucify Him**.*"* The nation of Israel will come to know Him as we have come to know Him. The cross that day has become the key to victory in the life of a believer. Calvary and the cross, is the key to all of humanity. It requires the Spirit of Revelation to see that this **3rd cross** is the key that unlocks the hearts and minds of all men. It was this **3rd cross** at the **3rd hour** that led to the **"*3rd Day,*"** resurrection day.

These things say,

He who is holy, He who is true, "He who has the <u>Key</u> of David, He who opens and no one shuts, and shuts and no one opens." (Revelation 3:7)

"Then it shall be in that day, That I will call My servant Eliakim (It is God who raises up) the son of Hilkiah (My portion comes from Jehovah); I will clothe him with your robe And strengthen him with your belt; I will commit your responsibility (government) into his hand. He shall be a father to the inhabitants of Jerusalem And to the house of Judah. "The Key of the house of David" I will lay on his shoulder; So he shall open, and no one shall shut; And he shall open, and no one shall shut. I will fasten him as a peg (nail) in a secure place, And he will become a glorious throne to his father's house. "They will hang on him all the glory of his father's house, the offspring and the posterity (Issues), all vessels of small quantity, from the cups to all the pitchers." "In that day," says the Lord of Hosts, the peg (nail) that is fastened in the secure place will be removed and be cut down and fall, and the burden that was on it will be cut off; for the Lord has spoken." (Isaiah 22:20-25)

In this passage of scripture, we see that the key of the house of David was the cross of Jesus. It was placed on His shoulder and all of its responsibilities as well. This key still remains the only key that can completely unlock all of man's troubles. He paid the price for our complete freedom. *"Whom the Son sets free is free in deed."* The word posterity or issue reveals that Jesus being a faithful high priest has been touched by the feelings of our infirmities. We all have issues, self created issues and ancestral issues, but we all have them. It doesn't matter where you're coming from, all that matters is where you're going. It doesn't matter what you have been through, all that matters is what you're willing to go through is the key. You might have been born underneath a bridge, the fact still remains that God has a plan through this door opening key for your life. He knows how many hairs we have on our head and how many we left on our pillow last night. He has never missed a sparrow's funeral. If the generation before you can not see that there is a way made to walk free of anything that might have attached itself to you and your family, you see it. It does not matter what the generation before you does with this key, it still will require two generations to break any curse. A generation that will come alive to the truth and a generation that can be trained with the truth. Let your generation be the generation that will come alive through this process, and then start investing into your children the principals of this key, the cross.

There shall come forth a rod from the stem of Jesse, And a branch shall grow out of his roots. (Isaiah 11:1)

A very powerful portion of scripture here that shows us the Messiah's intentions through this key, the cross. The stem that this prophet is referring to is the life of the Son of God, and the branch is His offspring. The word *"root"*, means heel, yes, the heel of your foot.

So the Lord God said to the serpent, verse 15, "And I will put enmity between you And the woman, and between your seed and her Seed;

He shall bruise your head, And you shall bruise His heel. (Genesis 3:14-15)

In the following scriptures, we will see that the cross has given every believer the key to authority to tread upon scorpions and serpents. The devil belongs in one place and one place alone in the life of a Christian, under their feet.

You shall trample the wicked, For they shall be ashes under the soles of your feet on the day that I do this, says the Lord of Hosts. (Malachi 4:3)

Then the seventy returned with joy, saying, "Lord, even the demons are subject to us in Your name." Behold, I give you the authority to trample on serpents and scorpions, and over all the power of the enemy, and nothing shall by any means hurt you." (Luke 10:17, 19)

"The Spirit of the Lord is upon Me, because He has anointed Me To preach the gospel to the poor; He has sent Me to heal the brokenhearted, To proclaim liberty to the captives And recovery of sight to the blind, To set at liberty those who are oppressed; To proclaim the acceptable year of the Lord." (Luke 4:18)

Notice that there is a semi-colon after the word poor. Where there is a punctuation mark like this, we know that a list of adjectives will follow: The brokenhearted, the captives, the blind and the oppressed. It was sin that has produced the effects of this poverty and it is the anointing that has broken every yoke and undone every burden. Jesus is our key to this victory. The cross, the key, has provided our way out. It is the cross or the key that has opened doors that could not be opened before, and shuts doors that could never be shut. The Jews would read from *"three"* scrolls when they would go into the synagogue and it took *"three"* years to finish each reading of these *"three"* scrolls. When Jesus stood up that day and read from the scroll of the Prophets, the second scroll, and then after His reading said that this scripture has been fulfilled in your hearing today. He was thrown out of the temple and they tried to stone Him. What they didn't realize is that they were throwing the *"3rd scroll"* out of the temple that day. The actual 3rd scroll was never read from that day, and from that day forward, Israel didn't receive Jesus as their Messiah. If we are not careful, we can judge what we do not fully understand, and miss what the Lord intends to change in our lives.

His parents went to Jerusalem every year at the feast of the Passover. And when He was twelve years old, they went up to Jerusalem according to the custom of the feast. When they had finished the days, as they returned, the Boy Jesus lingered behind in Jerusalem. And Joseph and His mother did not know it; but supposing Him to have been in the company; they went "days journey," and sought Him among their relatives and acquaintances. So when they did not find Him, they returned to

Jerusalem, (1 more days journey) seeking Him. Now so it was that after "three days" they found Him in the temple, sitting in the midst of the teachers, both listening to them and asking them questions. And all who heard Him were astonished at His understanding and answers. So when they saw Him, they were amazed; and His mother said, "Son, why have you done this to us? Look, Your father and I have sought you anxiously." (Luke 2:41-48)

Give us people in the local church that will begin to seek for the Lord once again in the house of God. People who are hungry for heaven sent answers and a heaven sent touch. The **"3rd Day"** is for such a people, people who are still anxiously looking for the government of God. Jesus is twelve at the time of this story; twelve in the bible is the number for government. He doesn't enter into public ministry until He is thirty. Eighteen years elapse between the years of twelve and thirty. Eighteen is the number in the Bible for "bondage". Government was letting the bondage of the religious order know that liberty from its system was coming. Somebody in the synagogue while Jesus was separated from his family, had to house and feed Him. I believe that there is a remnant people that has housed and fed the desire for a **"3rd Day"** move of God.

The move of God only deepens the order of the kingdom in the life of a believer. I stir you to seek after the Lord with all your heart. I also want you to know what you haven't been able to close in the past, and what you haven't been able to open in the present or the future, you need not look any farther than the cross. It still remains the key to all men's freedom. It is the Spirit of revelation that is in co-laborship with this key, the cross is what I feel God will use to allow all men to see a fresh need to come to Him. We have a church today because of their own lack of spirituality is very un-evangelistic. Today's believer does not come to church with expectation and anticipation wanting and waiting for the move of God. We have people today that when faced with truth from the Spirit of Revelation, by way of the Gifts of the Spirit, sit back and say, "we'll see." There was a time when people had reckless faith, a time when people would fast to see results, a time when people couldn't wait for Sundays to come. Faith doesn't sit back and say, I'll see. Faith is the substance of things hoped for, the evidence of things not seen. Faith is aggressive, tenacious, and bold. I believe that this **"3rd Day"** calling is opening the church to a fresh move of God, and by doing so, stirring our hearts to be anointed to reach our world. The present day church can not afford to fall further behind than where we are. If we are not careful, we might lose the chance to turn the tide of our generation. I know that there are many leaders today that feel that they do not know what to do to be affective in our present day. The Spirit of Revelation has a plan, God has always known how to reach people, and the day in which we live is no different. I will be sharing with you in the next chapter, ***Capturing the character of the "3rd Day"*** the reason we have seen three generations that have been half turned. The fact of the matter remains, Jesus is still the key. Jesus asked His disciples one day, *"who do men say that I am?"*

When Jesus came into the region of Caesarea Philippi, He asked His disciples, saying, "Who do men say that I, the Son of Man, am?" So they said, "Some say John the Baptist, some Elijah, and others Jeremiah or one of the prophets." He said to them, "But who do you say that I am?" Simon Peter answered and said, "You are the Christ, the Son of the living God." Jesus answered and said to him, "Blessed are you, Simon Bar-Jonah, for flesh and blood has not revealed this to you, but My Father who is in heaven." And I say to you that you are Peter and on this rock I will build My church, and the gates of Hades shall not prevail against it. "And I will give you the "KEYS" of the kingdom of heaven, and whatever you bind on the earth will be bound in heaven, and whatever you loose on earth will be loosed in heaven." (Matthew 16:13-19)

The Apostle Peter is now seeing through the Spirit of Revelation, what the nation of Israel is about to miss. When Jesus called him *"Simon Bar-Jonah."* Bar is this man's middle name, and Jonah was his father's name. Jesus was making sure that in Peter's mind, the information that was coming into his heart that day, was coming from His heavenly Father. Peter's name, *"Simon."* (Shama) is the same name that Simon the Cyrenian has. Once again we see through this Apostle, a movement that will draw attention to the cross for the rest of time. The Apostle Peter or *Simon,* (Shama) was given the responsibility of the ***"3rd Day."*** It was Peter (Shama) who saw Jesus Christ, for who He was.

When Jesus dealt with Peter's character, He always referred to him as Simon. We must realize that the very same thing happens with us in our relationship with the Lord. When God deals with our character, when He awakens us to and for more ability, He is calling to our destiny. It's the Spirit of Revelation that shows us our present day responsibilities of taking the cross in a **"3rd Day"** season, to our generation. The first thing that needs to happen is for the church to get a fresh look at the Lord themselves. The second thing that we all must be open to is, change for effectiveness. When the average life expectancy for church attendance of a new convert is only six weeks, something is wrong. Post modern society is looking for a genuine move of God. There's only one thing that they need, it's the cross. I feel that all that the church has experienced by way of movements in the past has prepared us to minister effectively to our present day. People still long to fill that void in their lives that only Jesus can fill. It was *Simon* that led the way to the upper room, and it was *Simon* (Shama) that lead the way to Cornelius house eleven years after Pentecost. Remember eleven is the number for disorder, it will be the Spirit of Revelation that will show us, those that are open for instructions, how to reach with effectiveness in our society. We have been in a place of disorder long enough and we can't stay there much longer. We are a people that stand the chance of being passed over and forgotten about, because of our own desire to do things our way, not **"His."**

The Spirit of Revelation is a timeless weapon, maximize its potential.

Chapter 10

"Capturing the Character of the 3rd Day"

"For it might have been sold for more than "three" hundred denarii and given to the poor." And they criticized her sharply. (Mark 14:5)

We live in a time where the words Apostle and Prophet are used too lightly. We have today many that are self appointed to these offices when they themselves know nothing about their true meaning. We have ministers that are more interested in popularity, the success of self promotion, than what really pleases the Father. We have pride, parades of coming into a service late and leaving early, and powerless meetings. We have highbred mentalities that think that they are one book, song or revelation away from national stardom. We have slick haired, shiny shoed, spineless preachers who preach on Sunday like their paycheck is depended upon on Friday. Not everyone who straps a collar around their neck and calls themselves "Bishop" is who they really say they are. We are given instructions in the book of **Revelation Chapter Two,** to test those who call themselves, "Apostles." Give us some real men and women of God who know how to come from the presence of prayer where they have met with Jesus. We cry out for authentic personalities that through their strong identify in Christ can connect us with life changing destiny in Christ. Men and women, who know how to pull us from the ditches of life and bring us into the glories of Zoë life. Give us ministers that know what pleases the Father and then pursues what is in their hearts with all of their strength. I hear people claiming the name of these offices, but I don't see anyone in the role of what produces the presence and the power of God. Jesus said, *"If you want to be great, learn to be the servant of all."* It is the heart of a servant that makes the old want to serve the young, the young to serve the old. It is the act of service that makes the rich serve the poor and the poor serve the rich. The educated serves the uneducated and uneducated serves the educated. The white man serves the black man and the black man serves the white man.

"...but the people who know their God shall be strong, and carry out great exploits." (Daniel 11:32)

It's in being a servant that you find out about the anointing of God. In this scripture above, we see what most ministries lack today which is the understanding of brokenness. A woman has entered the picture to anoint Jesus for His burial, I'm sure that she might not have fully understood what she was doing when she was doing it. But, never the less, she has broken an Alabaster flask of costly oil and has poured it on His head. All that is said about this situation is that it could have been sold for a lot of money and this money given to the poor. They considered what was done to be a waste. This oil was for her wedding night, the anointing of this **"3rd Day"** is for people who want communion with God in an intimate way. I see and meet so many ministers who do not see what they have needed to see to really be successful. Humility and brokenness is something that has eluded them from entering real ministry. When something is dropped and broken, you can not control the flow of that breakage. Anyone can spin off the top of a bottle and pour out what is wanted. We all can measure carefully what we want. But when something is broken, the flow is now out of control. This is something that I feel, we as believers, must always keep in mind. God wants a flow in today's church that can not be controlled. It will require brokenness, humility and a surrendering that will produce a fresh anointing. Humility is a product of intimacy and intimacy is the path to a fresh approach to God and man. Humility is not acting like a door mat; it's standing up with accountability and responsibility, saying, "Father, I surrender to Your counsel and Your ways." There have always been two types of ministers, ministers that serve the people and ministers that minister to the Lord.

"And the Levites who went far from Me, when Israel went astray, who strayed away from Me after their idols they shall be their iniquity. "Yet they shall be ministers in My sanctuary, as gatekeepers of the house and ministers of the house; they shall slay the burnt offering and the sacrifice for the people, and they shall stand before them to minister to them. "Because they ministered to them before their idols and caused the house of Israel to fall into iniquity, therefore, I have raised My hand in an

oath against them." says the Lord God, "that they shall bear their iniquity." "And they shall not come near Me to minister to Me as priest, nor come near any of My holy things, nor into the Most Holy place; but they shall bear their shame and their abominations which they have committed." (Ezekiel 44:10-13)

God says in this passage of scripture, that there will come a day that priest that are more interested in idols and mislead people will not have access to His presence. Not everyone you see on T.V. or speaking in a meeting where they might be used greatly at the present time, is God always well pleased. Could you imagine having so much money or lands and assets, that we think we can tell God what to do and expect Him to honor it and then do our own thing. We have had too many *"Good services."* I want to see changed lives, fruit that lasts and souls won to the Kingdom. Character and integrity is something that will out last time. I don't want to be a minister who is accepted at the moment by people and cut off from God's presence in the long run. Stubbornness is idolatry, and all stubbornness is, is the worship of your will and your way. I want to always be pleasing to the Lord. The anointing for a life time means more to me than all the tea in China. We as God's people must guard our hearts from pride; it has always been the path that leads to a fall. The Lord said to me,

"Capture the nature of this movement, if you don't, you will be doomed to become a people of rituals and routines all over again. You will require the movement to serve you and you

will never understand how to serve the movement."

For this reason, I, Paul, the <u>prisoner</u> (someone who has made up his mind through his service to not have a choice) of Christ Jesus for you Gentiles — if indeed you have heard of the dispensation of the grace of God which was given to me for you, how that by <u>revelation</u> (A laying , making naked, events by which things, states or persons withdrawn from view are made visible to all.) He made known to me the mystery (as I have briefly written already, by which, when you read, you may understand my knowledge in the mystery of Christ), which in other ages was not made known to the sons of men, as it has now been revealed by the Spirit of His holy, (a cut above) Apostles and Prophets; that the Gentiles should be fellow heirs, of the same body, and partakers of His promise in Christ through the gospels, of which I became a minister according to the gift of the grace of God given to me by the effective working of His power. To me, who am "less than" the least of all the saints, this grace was given, that I should preach among the Gentiles the unreachable riches of Christ. (Ephesians 3:1-8)

The Apostle Paul was an amazing man. If there was anyone celebrated in the New Testament outside the Life of Christ, it was Paul. He wrote two thirds of the New Testament and carried out what others should of finished, but didn't. He says something here that we must hear when he says that he was the least of the saints. I submit to you that this was not false humility in any way at all; it was an understanding within him that produced true anointing. Paul first of all knew that his anointing and calling was only as strong as his submission was to God's authority. At the first of the year, 2004, the Lord filled my heart with a message entitled, *"Authority and the Anointing, Government before Glory."* He shared with me the thing that Paul knew the most. His anointing was based on his understanding of authority. I meet people all over this nation that share with me how called, gifted and anointed they are. My first question to them is, where do you go to church and to whom are you submitted? Normally, if someone has a warped perception of the structure of God's government, they will say something like, "Jesus is the Lord of my life and I am the church, I don't need to go to a church to serve God." Really what they're saying is I'm stubborn, I'm an idol worshipper and I will do my own thing. These people who have God given abilities that never reach their fullness because of the lack of character to function at a higher level has never been worked out. It is in our relationships with people that we find out where Jesus is Lord and where He isn't. It is where He is Lord that we have grown to a level of maturity so that the anointing can minister as the anointing. And where He isn't Lord, is where we lack the anointing. By seeing where we still need to grow is where the lack of anointing is made known. But these types of revelations can only be discovered through our submission to do things the way the Lord would have us to do them. This type of development is first worked out in prayer, and then with people. It is impossible to have a correct relationship vertically with God and not have one horizontally with people. Prayer within its relationship with a believer has defining moments.

Then He came the "3rd Day" and said to them, "Are you still sleeping and resting?" It is enough! The hour has come. (Mark 14:41)

Within the relationship of prayer, the believer has time to awaken to truth and be ready to make things right. It is our relationship with people that reveals our relationship with the Lord. It is in our authoritative relationship with the Lord where we receive His anointing to be like him in the earth. True anointing is displayed through people who have His true heart. To have the heart of a servant is to have the heart of God. Ministers and laity as well need to have the heart of God to be truly anointed. Paul also knew a truth that we will look into in Chapter 11. He knew how to not let the last thing that God did in him and through him, to keep him from the next thing that the Lord wanted to do in him and through him. Apostles place in order and Prophets proclaim the word of the Lord. The present day need for the Apostles and the Prophets, are a must. We need Prophets like Samuel who heard from God and served faithfully for over forty years in guiding a nation. When Samuel was living with Eli, he had not heard the Lords voice before. His ear was untrained, but the Lord began to speak to him.

Now the boy Samuel ministered to the Lord before Eli. And the word of the Lord was rare in those days; there was no widespread revelation. And it came to pass at the "time," while Eli was laying down in his place, and when his eyes had begun to grow so dim that he could not see, Verse 7, (Now Samuel did not yet know the Lord, nor was the word of the Lord yet revealed to Him.) And the Lord called Samuel again the "3rd time." (I Samuel 3:1-2, 7-8)

Samuel acknowledged the Lord when the Lord called him the *"3rd time."* I feel in my heart that God has a people who have a desire to have a trained ear to hear him as He presently calls to the church of today. In a time where there is more repeated revelation than wide spread revelation, in a time where there is more disinterest than interest for the house of God, and in a time where we are not as excited about the word of the Lord as we once were. We need a fresh word from Heaven with which to mark our generation. One of the Prophet's responsibilities is to bridge the gap between generations.

"Behold, I send you Elijah the prophet before the coming of the great and dreadful day of the Lord. And he will turn the hearts of the fathers to the children, and the hearts of the children to their fathers, lest I come and strike the earth with a curse." (Malachi 4:5-6)

There were those that feel that this portion of scripture only deals with spiritual fathers and spiritual sons. I believe that mentoring is one of the most powerful things that can happen between generations. It is something that the Lord is doing in today's church, and it is working quite successfully. I feel that this passage does reflect this truth, but, it also speaks of generations coming together to produce a stronger core of people. It requires two generations to break any curse. A generation to come alive to a truth and a generation to train with the truth. The prophetic office through the spirit of revelation has been given this awesome responsibility. If sin can visit three to four generations, then why can't the strength and blessing of God? From Abraham to the sons of Levi, there were four generations. Abraham started the process of giving that can make each generation after it more successful than the one before it. Why don't we as Christians start charting and living through the mind of Christ, and in the spirit of revelation, in such a way that our children will live lives blessed beyond where we can take them? Each generation after Christ becoming Lord of that family, should be stronger in their commitment to the Kingdom. They should be much more financially successful than the previous generation, healthier, sounder in mind, and in all that Jesus has come to invade our lives with. I want to show you a truth about two families, Abraham's family and the family of God.

Ephraim has mixed himself among the peoples; Ephraim is a cake unturned. (Hosea 7:8)

Abraham is the great, great grandfather of Ephraim, and Ephraim is the son of Joseph. The word *mixed* is one of the words that define the *anointing*. Ephraim is a man that has tremendous potential, but follows the pattern of his past. Ask any pastor in America today that has seen and tried to pastor the last four generations. They will tell you what I'm about to tell you. The last four generations have been a people who have been for the most part, *"half turned."* We have a church today that has mixed herself so closely with the world, that we almost want world type standards in our spiritual life. There is a root problem in the life of Ephraim that exists in the life of the church today. It starts with the call of God on Abraham's life. Abraham's generation was a generation of conviction. God calls this man to leave his country, Ur of the Chaldees, and follow Him. Abraham was a moon worshipper, and the Lord God begins to show his generation His plan for it. The Lord tells Abraham that his descendants will be like the stars of the sky and the sand on the sea shore. Abraham is married to a woman who is barren, for this miracle to happen, it will require believing in hope against hope.

We see God doing a *"three"* generational miracle to honor His plan. Isaac's wife, and Jacob's wife were also barren and in need of a miracle. Abraham must have grown impatient with the Lords timing and try's to help God with His plan by having children with Hagar. What is so powerful about this story is that Isaac is the second born child of Abraham, Ishmael is his first born. We know that Ishmael is a product of this man's flesh, and still remains to this day a thorn in the flesh of man. Child psychologist will tell you that the second born child in a family is more aggressive by nature. I don't really understand why, maybe it is because the second born is compared to the first born. Maybe the second born feels that he or she has to live up to the first born accomplishments? I know as a parent that we try and love each of our children unconditionally. What we are about to embark on and by no means am I trying to say that the order of a household is any better than the other, there is something taking place with the second born children over the next *"three"* generations that show us a powerful spiritual truth. Abraham (**Genesis 21:22-34**), digs seven wells for the watering of his live stock. By **Genesis 26**, Isaac re-digs the wells of his father but makes the mistake of calling them what His father called them (**Genesis 26:18**). For the past twenty-five years, the body of Christ has been following this same pattern spiritually. Isaac, like the church, was not taught to dig his own wells. The church has been drinking from the wells of revelation of our fore fathers and we have fallen into a trap. We have failed in training each generation to discover God for themselves.

Every parent knows how important it is for our children to develop their own relationship with God. There comes a time in their lives that they are ready to leave home, and there comes a time in their lives where they can no longer for the most part, ride on the parents walk with God. As a parent, we also understand that you never stop being a parent you're always there for your children. But Isaac is now calling these wells what his father has called them. I am not suggesting that we disregard the studies and discoveries of our spiritual fathers, but if a generation comes and goes without knowing God for themselves, that generation will be weaker spiritually than the one before it. I see how this second born child, Isaac could have had the drive to have pursued things differently, but he didn't. Isaac has children of his own, and the Lord speaks to him that there were two nations in his wife's womb. God tells him that the older child, Esau will serve the second born child Jacob. Once again, opportunity knocks. Jacob begins down the path of the generation before him. Even though he has a wrestling match with God in **Genesis 32** and even though God does change his name twice, once in **Genesis 32**, when He calls him **Israel** and the other in **Isaiah 44:2**; when He calls him "Jeshurun." It means the Lord will straighten you out. God does touch this man and causes his walk to be different, but his home life is a reflection of his relationship with God. I don't want to sound judgmental, but this truth still remains. I wish ministers would wake up to the fact that we can only give spiritually to our congregations what we can give emotionally to our families. What we contribute to the family reveals the depth of truth that we have in our relationship with God.

Jacob had twelve children; his house was a house full of strife and jealousy. Joseph who is the eleventh born child begins to be dealt with by the Lord. Eleven is the number for disorder. Joseph is a prophetic picture of what I see the Lord doing in the church today. He spends most of his life trying to recover his father's household. And even thou he is used greatly, he never really has the time to develop all that God had for Him. Joseph begins to have children for himself and recognizes what I believe the church needs to see.

And Joseph said to his father, they are my sons, whom God has given me in this place. And he said, "Please bring them to me, and I will bless them." Now the eyes of Israel were dim with age, so that he could not see. Then Joseph brought them near him, and he kissed them and embraced them. And Israel said to Joseph, "I had not thought to see your face; but in fact, God has also shown me your offspring!" So Joseph brought them from beside his knees, and he bowed down with his face to the earth. And Joseph took them both, Ephraim with the right hand toward Israel's left hand, and Manasseh with his left hand toward Israel's right hand, and brought them near to him. Then Israel stretched out his right hand and laid it on Ephraim's head, who was the younger, and his left hand on Manasseh's head, guiding his hands knowingly, for Manasseh was the first born. (Genesis 48:9-14)

In the Old Testament, the first born received the birth right, the blessing. But, one again, we see order and tradition breaking so that God's plan can have preeminence. Ephraim, the second born child is now receiving Israel's blessing. Ephraim's name means, **'Double portion of fruit.'** And Manasseh's name means, **'To put an end to sorrow.'** I believe that God would have us to recognize that it will take a mark of maturity to embrace what He would like to do. I think that the body of Christ is developed enough to submit to doing things differently. We must set aside our pride and cling to a teachable spirit. Joseph realizes that each generation has grown weaker instead of stronger. He brings from behind his knees the next generation that has the same pattern as the last **"three"** and begins to reveal the truth. Joseph is making a statement here, he's saying, our family has been out of order too long. The church has been out of order long enough. For the last **"three"** generations, we have not taught the art of digging the wells of knowing God like we should have. We have not modeled servanthood and brokenness. We have not been a people of prayer and from that prayerful life, brought forth humility and anointing. As embarrassing as it might be, someone has to expose the truth. He is saying that he doesn't want to see another generation turn out *"Half turned."* For the last four generations, we have seen a people in the church that are half hearted towards the things of the Kingdom. I believe that this embarrassment and the source of its roots, are being uncovered. We must be aggressive with our pursuit of God's presence. We must place every generation that the Lord allows us to minister to, in touch with heavens revelation for their generation.

And he said, "Thus says the Lord: Make this valley full of ditches." (water canals) "For thus says the Lord: You shall not see wind, nor shall you see rain; yet that valley shall be full of water, so that you, your cattle, and your animals may drink." And this is a simple

matter in the sight of the Lord; He will also deliver the Moabite into your hand. (2 Kings 3:16-18)

The King of the Moabites has just broken covenant with the King of Israel, and the King of Israel has rallied support from the King of Judah. Both of their armies have been walking towards the battle, in full battle array for a week. They are dressed for the battle, but something is wrong, they have no water to drink. Jehoshaphat says:

"Is there no prophet of the Lord <u>here</u> that we may inquire of the Lord by him?" (2 Kings 3:11)

The prophet Elisha tells them to dig water canals and they would see the deliverance of the Lord. I want to tell you the same thing, if we will dig the wells of revelation for ourselves, and be willing to train the next generation to do the same, we can recapture the presence and power of God once again. We might think that we are ready for the battle all dressed up in our armor, but without water, we can only last so long. It is a *simple matter*, no prayer, no water, no water, no strength.

Each of Abraham's descendants had the ability to produce a double portion, none of them did. We need to see the strength in Christ that we have as an inheritance, and then convey it to the next generation to be stronger than what we have turned out to be. If we do not pursue the Lord now for the sake of this generation's revelation, we will repeat history instead of writing history.   Our future depends upon our present hour obedience. Obedience has always been and will always be the foundation of our deliverance. Let's go after this new hour and this new age with all of our hearts.

Chapter 11

Chasing After the Presence of the 3rd Day

So they departed from the mountain of the Lord on a journey of "three days;" and the ark of the covenant of the Lord, went before them for the "three days" journey, to search out a resting place for them. (Numbers 10:33)

As I travel throughout America, I have met so many people who are frustrated by little to no move of God in their church services, and a lack of the manifestation of the presence of the Lord. In my own prayer life, I have felt like I was running into a wall every time I would go to Him in prayer. After *"three"* months of this, I began to ask the Lord, what was taking place. He told me that I had come to an end of an age. He went on to say, that there was more of Him available if I was willing to step to another level. He shared a portion of scripture with me that has completely changed my heart and life. In **(Song of Solomon 2:14)**, the Word says,

O my dove, in the clefts of the rock, In the secret places of the cliff, let me see your face, Let me hear your voice; For your voice is sweet, And your face is lovely.

The church must understand that the frustration that most of us are feeling and have felt, I believe is heaven sent. The Lord said to me, that this frustration will produce the right type of fruit in the hearts of the Bride. We must also realize that we are preaching to generations that have never experienced revival. They are not old enough to remember the Charismatic renewal movement. But I am not that far removed from the last great move of God and I can't remember. During this movement services, were held for seven to ten days in length, and there would be *"three"* sessions every day. Each of these services would be packed out with hungry people for more of the Lord. People were ignited by revelation from the Word of God that stirred them to pray, praise and preach to family and friends about what they had discovered. I remember that people would leave their bibles on chairs or pews to guarantee that they would have a seat for the next service. People would travel states and even countries to be in seminars. Today we find it hard to get people to come to church on Wednesday nights. We have completely eliminated Sunday night services, and we schedule meetings that do not go any longer than three days. We have had *"three"* generations since this last move of God, that desperately need to encounter God for themselves. The first thing that is stated here in this portion of scripture is the word **"dove."** Solomon refers to his bride as a dove. In **Chapter 1:15**, he says, **"You have dove's eyes."** We know that the Holy Spirit is referred to as a dove. **(Matthew 3:16)** But, most people don't know that doves do not have peripheral vision. They can not see out the corners of their eyes. Their vision is on what is in front of them, Jesus said,

"The lamp of the body is the eye. If therefore your eye is single, or good, your whole body will be full of light." (Matthew 6:22)

Today, we have a society that pulls on our lives in many different ways. The Kingdom of God desires to be the main gravitational pull. We must train our hearts, and the people's hearts that are around us, to make Jesus our most important focus. When we do so, nothing takes the place of Jesus being first. Wednesday night services or whenever a service is scheduled, our attendance is the fruit of this correct priority.

We also see that he desires to meet with her in the ***"secret places of the stairs."*** Ask any contractor about how stairs are built, and they will say that from one level to the other, there must be risers. To go from one level to another, you must first run into a riser and let that riser compel you to step up. I believe that spiritually, the church has done just that. The frustration that we are feeling is nothing more than the church coming to the end of an age, and also heaven calling us to step to another level. If we stay where we are, we will continue to run into that wall, or riser, and one of two things will take place. We will either stop our pursuit for the Lord, and choose to go back to an old Word and the frame work of an old move, or we will see that God's voice and His face can be experienced a fresh. This enclosure with God almighty is what we all need. In **(Genesis 5:21-24)**, we see, ***Enoch walked with God "three hundred" years,*** in verse twenty four, ***And Enoch walked with God; and he was not,***

for God took him. There are Jewish writings that tell us that Enoch desired to have a talk with his great, great, great, great grandfather Adam. They also reveal that Adam was a man that spent weeks separated in caves under great oppressions of depression. I'm sure that when Adam found himself depressed like this, it was because he was remembering what it was like walking with the creator of the heavens and the earth. These writings tell us that Enoch desired to talk with his relative about what this walk with God was like. Enoch was sixty five at the time, after his conversation with Adam, the bible says, **Enoch walked with God "three Hundred" years.** He heard something; he saw something about the way Adam talked about this walk with God that made him desire this walk for himself. I want to remind you that the number **"three"** speaks of resurrection, trinity, but also eternity. The only way that we can see our next step in Him, is through the eyes of revelation. The call of the Holy Spirit on this generation is the same call that entered the heart of Enoch. There is a desire coming from the throne of God to this present day generation for intimacy. I feel that God wants this generation to know what revival really is. I have been blessed to be part of exceptional moves of God that have only left me hungering for more of them. In **(Genesis 1:11-13)**, we find that God created seed that would reproduce after its own kind. He created the seed of impartation into a generation that has never seen the Lord in His fullness. We need to make a deposit into the lives of the people who have never tasted the presence of the Lord and have no real knowledge of His power. There is a people in place that do not know for themselves the benefits that come when Jesus and the work of the Kingdom come first. A people who need to see God's strength through reconciling a marriage that seems to be beyond saving. A God that heals to the uttermost, a God that will turn the worst of the worst situations around and show you that there is nothing that is too great for Him! A God that already has a way made known before you arrive at a place in life where you think there is no way at all. There are so many that have never developed this type of relationship, and faith with the Lord. A faith that calls you to deny any other report than what the Word of God has to say. Something that calls you to weekly fasting and daily communion with Him in prayer and the study of His word. A zeal that comes from an over flow that compels you to share Jesus publicly and pray for those that will allow you to pray and believe for them.

We have a generation alive today that does not know the importance of the development of the fruit or the out come of the Spirit. Love, joy and peace that against such is no law. A law that conquers insecurity and releases someone to have the right confidence to live large and accomplish something great. A God that declares **greater is He that is within you, than he that is after you**. (Authors version) We need to make a deposit in a people who will pursue His presence and come to know Him. A people who will trust His counsel and His ways because they are submitted to a God that they know, knows what He is talking about. A generation that follows a God of real guidance that will lead them into real stability and success. We do not have the same ambition in today's church that we once had, but this does not mean that He has changed. The church has changed, and our present day condition is evident of how far we have gravitated away from His likeness.

Our pursuit to grow a church in size and not in character has left us looking for answers everywhere but in the Word of God. He is a friend that sticks closer than a brother to those that will keep His commandments, and regard Him as first in their lives. **(John 15:14-15)** We need a people who have a desire to reproduce after what the Lord desires for the twenty first century. In **(Luke 2:41-50)**, we see that Jesus' family went to Jerusalem for the custom of a feast. It was a full day's journey to Jerusalem from where they lived. It was a full day's journey home as well, but when they had returned from the city they realized that Jesus was not with them, so they had to travel back to this city to find Him. They are now in **"the 3rd Day"** of their travels. The text says, **"after three days they found Him in the temple."** When they arrived in Jerusalem, they found Him in the temple sitting in the midst of the teachers. He was there because He was now twelve years of age and by custom required to be there. Twelve is the number of government and by being in the temple, he was announcing to the present day religious order that things would soon be changing. Before we go any farther, we must also see that while He was separated from His natural parents, somebody had to house Him, and take necessary care of Him. There is a remnant people who have hung on to the belief that the move of God is what people need. We have housed the idea, and fed the thought to a generation that Jesus, and coming to know Him in an intimate way, is what holds the key to complete victory and personal success. The text goes on to say, **"your father and I have sought You anxiously."** I believe that the intimacy that the Holy Spirit wants with the present day believer, will stir their hearts to seek after God, in His house, anxiously. I want to tell the religious order of our day that God's government will prevail. You might be having a moment of success without Him, but His will, His word and His work, will be what people inevitably seek after. Jesus did not step into public ministry until He was thirty years of age. Eighteen years ago, (eighteen is the number of bondage); the bondage of religion has always been broken by the government of God. "**The 3rd Day"** is starting to excite a people to see and seek after the Lord again.

Solomon tells us that from these secret places comes many things.

My beloved is like a gazelle or a young stag. Behold he stand behind our wall; He is looking through the windows, Gazing through the Lattice. My beloved spoke, and said to me; "Rise up, my love, my fair one, And come away. For lo, the <u>winter</u> is past, the rain is over and gone. The flowers appear on the earth; The time of the singing has come, And the voice of the <u>turtledove</u> is heard in <u>our land</u>. Song of (Solomon 2: 9-12).

The word **lattice** is the same word that is used for the word **windows**, in **(Malachi 3)**. God said test Me in this, the tithe, if I will not open up the windows of heaven and pour out for you such blessings that there will not be room enough to receive it. **(Malachi 3:10)** I feel that the Lord has been watching through the lattice or window to see who has been willing to pass the test, the test being faithfulness. I personally know so many people who have strayed from their roots of faith. People who once moved in the power of God, and now think it is for a side room, and no longer for the public service. People who have become more interested in what others think, than what God thinks. I believe God is watching, and the one's who have not compromised, are the one's who will shine in this next season. Notice that he says, *"the winter has passed."* He is talking of spiritual bareness, and little to no move of God. He goes on to say, *"And the voice of the turtledove is heard in our land."* This refers to people being anointed with a prophetic word. Revelation can come through one source and one source alone, that is through the Holy Ghost. I know in my heart that God wants to give to a generation a rhema word that will recover, restore and resurrect us beyond other movements.

In **Chapter 2, verse sixteen**, he says, *"He feeds his flock among the lilies."* **Verse Two refers to the Easter season**. Easter of course is the celebration of *"the 3rd Day."* The resurrection of Christ. He's telling us that God feeds His people through revelation because of *"the 3rd Day"* resurrection. I want you to see that He plants lilies among thorns.

"Now these are the ones sown among thorns; they are the ones who hear the word, and the cares of his world, the deceitfulness of riches, and the desires for other things entering in choke the word, and it becomes unfruitful." (Mark 4:18-19)

The church has had the life of the Word of God choked out by the cares of the world, the deceitfulness of riches, and by the desires for other things. There are reasons for this that I will share with you in the next chapter. But, the fact still remains, that God has planted, and then feeds His people through resurrection power, by way of revelation of His Son. These three things that the enemy uses to distract people, does not have to affect you. You can be just like Solomon's bride in **Chapter One, verse Four,** *"draw me away"* and *"we will run after you."* It is very evident that God is calling His people to Him. But who has ears to hear Him?

Who is this coming up from the wilderness, leaning upon her beloved? (Song of Solomon 8:5).

I'll tell you who it is, a frustrated people. We have leaned upon our own self reliance to long. We have ridden on past revelations, and on stories of God moving in other times. There is a people that are on the rise and coming out of a spiritual season of wilderness right now, they are a people who are leaning on Him. I encourage you to stay faithful, the coming revival will be worth it. In the year 2000, I had an open vision. For those of you that know me, you know that I don't run around and say, *"the Lord said this to me or the Lord showed me that."* I'm very careful about making sure that what I share publicly is true, and accurate.

I saw the earth under the glory of God. Sin and sickness had been paralyzed for a season, and miracles were coming forth like a common thing. **The power of God was on display before the world just as I imagined.** Mass revival was taking place on all continents. At first, I thought I was given a special view at the millennial reign of the church. Then I noticed that all false religions had lost their grip on humanity and people by the masses were coming to Jesus to be their Lord and Savior. I feel this vision was given to me to prepare me for what is to come. I also feel that God is breathing on a people in a new way to connect them with Him in greater depth. Please realize that God is not required to breath into anything that He Himself has not formed.

My pastor, David Garcia, of the Grace Dome, at Brooksville Assembly of God, encouraged me to document this vision. Our best days are growing closer to us by the second, please stay on course.

Chapter 12

The Right Heart for The 3rd Day

So I came to Jerusalem and was there "three days." then I arose in the night, I and a few men with me; I told no one what my God had put in my heart to do at Jerusalem. (Nehemiah 2:11)

In this last and final chapter, I want to reiterate the importance of a right spirit to do the right job, in *"the 3rd Day."* I see so many self appointed people who claim to be something that I'm not quite sure they understand. People who have the spirit of the past wrapped up in the titles of the twenty-first century move of God. I say again, *we must be a people who have captured the nature of the present day move of God. If we aren't, we will require the movement to serve us, and we will not know how to serve the movement.* The system is changing, our hearts are changing. Please remember this about your walk and likeness in God, it's all about change. Success in the future work of the Holy Ghost depends on our willingness to change and always become more like Him. *"The 3rd Day"* is not about what we can receive from the Lord, it's about what we can do for the work of the Kingdom. In **(Genesis 39),** Joseph is wrongfully imprisoned. In this time of captivity, he meets two men from the palace of Pharaoh, one a butler, and the other a baker. Both men have dreams that trouble them, and

Joseph is there to interpret those dreams. He tells the butler, that the **three** vines that he has seen in his dream represent, **three days**. He lets him know, that within **three days**, he will be back in his rightful position, serving the King again. He also tells the baker, that within **three days** he will lose his life. I want to boldly encourage all the ministries that have been going through a process over the last five years. I know that it would have been easier to jump on the band wagon and gone in a more convenient way. But, it will be the ministries that have not compromised over this lean spiritual time that will arise in the year of 2005. When judgment is coming to other places and other people to turn their hearts back to what you never turned away from, you will shine. I feel that God will honor those who have stayed true, and have been faithful. It was the butler who was now back in his rightful place of serving the King.

Jesus tells us in...

(John 15:1), *"I am the true vine, and My Father is the vine dress."*

He tells us, that every branch that does not bear fruit, He will take it away. The word ***"takes"*** means He lifts up. A branch cannot bear fruit lying on the ground. There have been those that have tried to meet and minister to the world on their level. By no means should we act or lie to the world, that we are any better or superior than they are. We need to know how to meet them where they are, and lift them to a higher way of life. There are those who have suggested that we place a demand on humanity to be saved, but place no requirements on them to conform and be transformed into the image of Christ. There are those who would say, **_"that's the way you might have learned how to serve God, but don't place me in your box or under your control."_** Please let me save you a season of unnecessary frustration and grief. The principal and the process for all of us remains the same, but the way you might express this process can be different than others. Make no mistake about it, the end result, and the fruit for all of us, will look like Jesus if we have done things His way. Just as this branch must be lifted up, tied to a higher place *(the cross of Calvary)* and washed, we cannot bear fruit on the level we were at, prior to being saved. In this passage of scripture, we find **three** types of fruit. No fruit, more fruit, and much fruit. I believe if we will follow the following disciplines, we will be a people bearing the **3rd** type of fruit stated here. The best way to bear fruit is to hunger and thirst for the presence of the Lord. Moses was a man that once he found the presence of the Lord, nothing else satisfied him. We see a powerful example of this in the book of Exodus, Chapter **thirty three**. The people of God, start complaining once again about the way God is doing things after their deliverance from the land of Egypt. God calls these people who have seen His heart towards them, as well as His hand of blessing, *hard hearted and stiff necked.* How do people who have been through so much and seen the goodness of the Lord in such a powerful way, get like this? It is simple, a lack of His presence in their lives. Moses lived in Egypt the majority of his younger life. He was educated by the best that his scholars had to offer. He wore the best, ate the best, and lived in the best of Egypt. But, when he experienced the presence of the Lord, he was changed forever.

In this passage of scripture, God tells Moses that He will give these people a land that He has promised them, but they will have it without Him. Moses can't believe what he heard. Remember that they are in the middle of the desert, and Moses replies to God, that unless God goes with them, he, Moses, plans on staying right where the Lord stays.

In Moses' eyes, the desert was looking better with God and His presence, than anything Egypt had to offer. The people who have just been delivered have spent the last four hundred and thirty years in bondage, poverty and extreme hardship didn't see it that way. They wanted what God had promised them, a land of their own. What they want is the promise that the Lord made to them, and they wanted it now. Why were their hearts so cold? A lack of God's presence in their lives! They had not been spiritually, where Moses has been with the Lord. The minute we stop going into the presence of the Lord to fellowship with Him and receive His instructions into our hearts, the promises of God will be more important to us than His presence. We have many like the children of Israel in the church today. They want the promises of God more than the presence of God, and we wonder why we end up the way we end up. It is in His presence we're to stay pliable to His Will and His Word. We must stay patient to His timing and rely completely in trust and dependency on Him. We need a people who are so established in His ways, nothing can move us from His acts. If you ever find yourself in a season of delay, God is allowing this season for your benefit. Everything that He does in our lives turns us to Him and not away from Him. There are too many people in today's church that think that they are ready for revival, when in reality, we are not broken enough. You might be saying, *"not broken enough?"* I'm frustrated, my finances have hit bottom, and I'm being stretched in ways I have never thought possible. I feel that revival will not hit the body of Christ, until we get to the place of such surrenderance that we will not try and be in control any longer. We must arrive at a place with Him, that we do not try and take charge of after a season of breakthrough and victory. We must stay focused and thankful. A people that have learned to praise Him in whatever place they find themselves. I think we might have a long way to go!

Secondly, being committed to the right things is a must. When the church does not have the same burden to reconcile the world to the Father, the way Jesus had the passion to, tells us something. I want to share with you one more time, that **the "3rd Day,"** the **spirit of revelation**, is a divine call to the present believer to see life and the work of the Kingdom, through the eye's of the Holy Ghost. **Three** represents, resurrection, trinity and **eternity.** It is impossible to be about the Fathers' business, without a heart that is trained by grace instead of various trials. **(1 Peter 1:6)**. Dying is the best way to live!

Most assuredly, I say to you, unless a grain of wheat falls in to the ground and dies, it remains alone; but if it dies, it produces "<u>much grain</u>" (or fruit) He who loves his life will lose it, and he who hates his life in this world will keep it for eternal life. (John 12:24-25)

When Jesus went to the cross and died for our sins, He released to us, after the born again experience, His divine nature. **(2 Peter 1:4).** It should be in the heart of every believer, to want to die to this life and live life whole heartedly for the work of the Kingdom. We all have assignments, purposes and destiny to fulfill. Jesus' death and resurrection has produced salvation for each generation from Calvary to our present day. I want you to think about the multi-millions of people who have been saved through one man's obedience. Because He let the Father have His way, humanity has been altered forever. Each one of us has the God given ability to mark and reach our generation. There is a huge difference between the church's heart, and the Father's heart. When I look at the church and the fruit that it bares, and I look at the life of Christ and the fruit that He bore, something is wrong. Where the church is presently reveals what we want and what we desire. But, what might be wrong cannot be changed until we are willing to openly confess what we lack. We lack God patterned structure. The first way that the Lord begins to bring forth *"much fruit"* *in* our lives is through *conviction, discipline and being teachable*. We can only be trusted to the point that we are teachable. God's actions are all intended to push us towards the life and character we desire, but, can't reach without His help and assistance. It's the lack of fruitfulness in our lives that should place a deep desire to pursue Him with all of our hearts.

"And you have forgotten the exhortation which speaks to you as to sons:" **"My son, do not despise the chastening of the Lord, Nor be discouraged when you are rebuked by Him; For whom the Lord loves He chastens, And scourges every son whom He receives."** **(Hebrews 12:5-6)**

Now no chastening seems to be joyful for the present, but painful; never the less, afterward it yields the peaceable fruit of righteousness to those who have <u>trained</u> by it. (Hebrews 12:11)

For the grace of God that bring salvation has appeared to all men, <u>teaching</u> us that denying ungodliness and worldly lusts, we should live soberly, righteously, and godly in the present age.

When we become a people who have been trained by the grace of God, a people who really understand the nature of grace, we will live for what is right. One of the most important things that grace teaches us is we are free to live life right. When Jesus told the woman who was caught in adultery, **_"neither do I condemn you, go and sin no more."_** He wasn't just scolding her and letting her off the hook. He was birthing in her heart the nature of grace. She knew that according to the law, she was guilty, but according to grace in her heart, she was free never to return to any other life style other than following Jesus. She now knew what it was like to be free to make right choices. If we really understand being born again and being lead by the Spirit, we are free to follow Jesus and live completely for Him. We no longer live for ourselves or live life through our own eyes and after our own opinions. We can become a people who only want what He wants and a people who are willing to go and do whatever He desires. I want to be the person that brings forth the **3rd** type of fruit, ***much fruit.***

When we are trained by the nature of grace, we have a burden for what He is burdened for. We love the way He loves, we look at things the way He looks at things, and we express ourselves the way He expresses Himself. When Jesus was reaching people in His public ministry, especially when there were Pharisees involved, He tried to reach the person in need, and the religious person who couldn't see the person in need, the way Jesus saw them. The Pharisees were hard and cold because they lacked God's presence and His true nature in their ministries. Take the story found in **(Luke 7:36-50),** for example. Jesus is having lunch in one of the Pharisees house. He is approached from behind by a woman who is a prostitute. She begins to wash His feet with her tears, *(Her heart)* and dry them with the hair of her head. All the Pharisee can think is,

This man, if He were a prophet, would know <u>who</u> or <u>what</u> manner of woman this is who is touching Him, for she is a sinner. (Luke 7:39b)

The world has a standard for acceptance. It is based on who you are and what you have. This attitude of heart is not part of the new nature. This Pharisee can not see what Jesus can see about her. He can only hold her to her past actions and life style, he has a critical spirit. A critical spirit goes by first impressions, and first impressions with a critical spirit, are lasting impressions. Have you ever met someone or been in a certain fellowship of people that no matter how you have changed or how far you have come in your walk with God, they still remember you when or where. This spirit looks at the external, and not the internal. God on the other hand looks at the heart. This is why there is hope for the murderer, the wife beater, the drug user and the drunkard. There are many of us who think that we will never be any different than the way we are now. This is a lie from the enemy. All that needs to happen is for God to speak one Word, or bring us into a new season and what had a hold of us, we now have a hold of it. He opens our life by exposing us to His life and begins His change. Jesus let the Pharisee know how far his heart had drifted from the likeness of His Fathers. He said to him...

Then He turned to the woman and said to Simon, "Do you see this woman? I entered your house; you gave me no water for my feet, but she has washed my feet with her tears and wiped them with the hair of her head. You gave me no kiss, but this woman has not ceased to kiss My feet since the time I came in. Therefore I say to you, her sins which are many, are forgiven, for she loved much. But to

**whom little is forgiven, the same loves little."
Then He said to her, "Your sins are forgiven."
(Luke 7:44-48)**

There was a Jewish custom at this time that provided every guest with foot washing, a kiss and your head was to be anointed. There was also a process to this custom. If you were looked at by the host as being royalty, the host washed your feet. If you were looked at, as being equal to the host, his servants washed your feet. But, if you were looked at being less than the host, you washed your own feet. If you were looked at as lesser than, you were kissed on the cheek, equal to, on the hand, royalty, on the feet. The same process was used for being anointed. (**The above information came from Pastor David Garcia**). The Pharisee had provided none of these services for his guest, Jesus.

When you and I stop washing His feet with our hearts, it will be impossible for us to see victory for our lives. If we can not see victory for ourselves, how can we have the right kind of compassion for others? Our hearts must once again be encountered with the power of the Holy Ghost and our lives must once again by directed by the grace that saved us. If we will surrender afresh to the vision of the Holy Ghost, then He will have liberty to release to us His strategy for this generation.

The second thing that is necessary for success is *a heart of compassion.* Jesus said,

"For as Jonah was three days and three nights in the belly of the great fish, so will the Son of Man be three days and three nights in the heart of the earth." (Matthew 12:40)

The Scribes and Pharisees want to see a sign from Jesus to prove to them that He was the Messiah. To be completely honest with you, they really didn't care who Jesus was claiming to be. They had already rejected Him in their hearts. They wanted a performance. If you study the Word of God, you will find that even though signs and wonders will draw men and women, they will not change someone's heart. What Jesus did through the sign of the prophet Jonah, has given to all of us the ability to believe and over come this life, as Jesus did. But, let us quickly look at the life and times of the Prophet Jonah, and see why Jesus used him for an example. Jonah has been the subject of many different sermons down through the years but make no mistake about it, Jonah was God's man. God knew that Jonah was the man that could get the job done. God knew that his gifting and the anointing that He allowed to rest upon him, was well able. The city of Nineveh wasn't Jonahs first job. He comes from a ministry background that has spanned for over forty years. For the King of Nineveh and the people of this city to react as quickly as they did, tells us that they either know Jonah, or they know of him. Jonah prophesied in the time of the prophets, Amos and Hosea. They all taught at the school of the prophets together. God used this man in Jeroboam's days to restore kingdoms. **(2 Kings 14:25)** But now, we see that Jonah cannot see past the God given assignment of Nineveh. When it came to Nineveh, something was wrong. God knew what was in the heart of the prophet and it was time for the prophet to find out what God already knew about him. God knows that it's in the heart of every believer and if I can be bold with you for a moment, it just seems not to be in the churches heart to be completely obedient to God.

Our Father knows when, where and what to allow to happen in our lives for us to see and overcome what we need to see and overcome. Nineveh was God's perfect assignment to work his perfect work in His man. The word Jonah means **"Dove"**, but when it came to Nineveh, we see the prophet looking and acting like a serpent. Listen, prophets are hard enough to be around, much less an angry prophet. Something is fueling this prophet. I have tried to look for research concerning Jonah's life, but I have been unsuccessful. I don't know if this present condition in his life came from his childhood or along the way of his ministry. All I know is that God knows it is time to heal. If Jonah is to be completely obedient to God, he must heal. I have learned over the years that anger is a detection of what is really wrong in our lives. Jonah comes from a region called Gath-helher. This word means: **"A wine press, to make music, to paw, to search out, and to seek."** What is this telling us? Jonah is a problem solver no matter what the pressure has been like in the past. Jonah, up to this point in his life and ministry has sought out and searched for an answer. There are things in life that will come our way that no matter how successful or powerful you think you are or have become, they will humble our hearts. When God breaks ground in areas of our lives that have never experienced His grace, there is a season of insecurity and uncertainty. It is in these times and seasons of our walk with God, we find acceptance and unconditional love that breaks down walls of reservations and fear. Jesus told the Scribes and Pharisees that no other sign was needed for them than the sign of Jonah. He was telling them **the "3rd Day"** was what they needed. Jonah was an isolationist. He believed that salvation was for the Jews only. Through the following affliction, things are about to change in him. He is about to take a journey to experience and find God's embracing love.

Jonah is running from Nineveh. He was really running from the change that he now knew God needed to do in his life. He knows God! He also knew that if the people of Nineveh repented at the preaching of Jonah, God would spare them from judgment. What is under the surface of this story is that the eye can not see until the right situation presents itself? The people of Nineveh were killing off the Jewish people and Jonah wanted God to retaliate. In Chapter One of the book of Jonah, we see a disobedient prophet running from God and then punished. The scripture says,

"But Jonah arose to flee to Tarshish from the presence of the Lord." (Jonah 1:3)

As you study this small book, you will see this same statement more than once. When we want to avoid the touch of God in our lives, we try and stay as far from the Lord as we possibly can. But, when you and I leave the presence of the Lord, trouble will follow.

So he paid the fare, (Jonah 1: 3b).

We have been a people who have known the presence and power of God. We are also a people who are preaching every week to a people who have never been exposed to this type of ministry. There is a price to pay for obedience as well as disobedience. Please, once again, no matter what the humanists are saying, people are looking for what God can only do for them. Let us be a people who will rise up and lead a generation, and other generations who have fallen away from the Lord's presence, back into His glory and grace. Understand as Jonah's disobedience brought trouble to people around him, so will yours. You bring the fruits of hell instead of the fruits of heaven everywhere you go. Could you imagine being on board a ship with someone who's relationship with God is causing my stuff, your things to get thrown over board? Be a leader – not a follower. You were born an original, why die a copy. Jonah thought that he could escape his troubles by hiding in the bottom of the ship.

The scripture tells us,

But the Lord sent out a great wind, (Jonah 1:4a).

We realize through our past relationships and encounters with the Lord that He is patient. Make no mistake about it He will do whatever it takes to get our lives on track with His Will. God sent the storm. Yes, I said God sent the storm. When the Father is after you, you can run, but you can't hide. Trouble will be the thing that He uses to surface us and bring us back to Him. I pray that we do not have to hit bottom like Jonah. God does know how broken we need to be in order for us to let Him have His way in our lives.

In **Chapter Two**, we see a praying prophet running back to God and delivered. Jonah is now in the belly of a great fish. He has been carried to the bottom of the ocean by this fish and he feels like he is drowning. *(Look at Jonah 2:3-9)* Something very powerful happens. It's found in verse four:

"Then I said, I have been cast out of your sight; Yet, I will look again toward Your holy temple."

He knows in his heart the time clock within him tells him that the sun is going down and I will and must worship you. Jonah is at the bottom of the ocean. I pray that we do not have to sink this low before we return to the Lord's presence and His plan. When God entombs us, like Jonah is entombed by an ocean of problems, He forces us to fulfill His Will. He brings us to a place of no resistance and reveals to us that He is our complete and only resource. It is through refinement due to disobedience, that sin is stopped. When pottery is being cured in a furnace, the potter knows when to take the creation out of the fire. When the pot after being banged on, it responds with a sound called singing. Jonah's heart is now over riding his head. The present day believer is no different. I believe that our hearts in this **"3rd Day"** hour is over riding our desires for other things, other than Him. **In verses eight and nine, Jonah** says;

Those who regard worthless idols, forsake their own mercy. But I will sacrifice to you with the voice of thanksgiving; I will pay what I have vowed. Salvation is of the Lord.

Jonah realizes that his idol has been himself. His Will and his way have been more important than Gods. I think that the present day shape of the church is a clear indicator of these same choices. We all realize that things can no longer keep going the way they have. We are at the end of the rope. We have arrived at a dead end street. God lets His prophet discover that his strength is found in his praise. No matter where you are at right now, no matter what you are facing right now, God is in, and will inhabit your praise. You are one cry, shout or expression of praise away that will get your Father's attention and make that great fish, season of trouble, make it do a hard right turn and bring you to the place of being back on track. Praise is something that the Lord has given to us to be militant. It is something with which we war. It is something that makes all the efforts of the enemy to be completely paralyzed. It is something that is intercessory. Let a war cry come from the depth of your heart today. Make war on the floor with a crazy praise that places a fear of a turn around in the heart of the devil. The people of Jesus' day were starting to praise His ministry in such a way, attention that was normally on the Pharisees, was now on Jesus. I think it should be the same way today. The attention should be on Jesus and Jesus alone. But, you would be surprised how many ministries feel the same way the Pharisees felt. How many ministries today do you know that would rather keep people dependant upon them than on Jesus. They might not openly admit to this, but, a ministry that is secure in their assignment with God raises people up beyond leader's maturity, only to let people go onto their personal fulfillment.

Jonah in **Chapter Three** becomes a *faithful prophet* running with God and *rewarded.* Jonah is now in Nineveh and he prophesies the Word of the Lord. He leaves the city and watches and waits in hope that the people will not respond to the Word given by the prophet. One hundred and twenty thousand people repent at the hearing of this prophecy and Jonah is more interested in fulfillment of his prophecy than God sparing thousands of people from destruction. Nineveh is the greatest revival recorded in the Word of God.

If ministers today are not careful, they can become just as insensitive as Jonah. We can become more interested in what we want and believe in concerning how things should go than what God desires. Ministers can do something so long that they do most of what they do without God. I do not want what "might be" in me, to keep me from being apart of one of the greatest moves of God in the earth.

In **Chapter Four,** we find an angry prophet running ahead of God and rebuked. Jesus used Nineveh's repentance to chide His unrepentant contemporaries. He needed to use no other source than the life of Jonah to point out the condition of the Scribes and Pharisees. In the first verse of **Chapter Four,** God repents of His plan to destroy this city and Jonah is upset with God's mercy. The Lord asked Jonah, *"Is it right for you to be angry?" (Verse 4)*

Jonah is now on the east side of the city and he is watching to see what will happen. In the process, the Lord causes a plant to grow over the prophet to provide shade for him. Jonah is very thankful to have shade and comfort from the hot sun. A worm comes the following day and begins to eat the plant in such a way that just as fast as the plant sprung up to shade and comfort him, it has faded just as fast. The prophet is furious about how uncomfortable he has become because he has lost his former covering. He is now exposed again. Jesus is using this prophet's life to share with them that He will be a stone in their bed of discomfort until they can see people the way He can. Jesus is telling them that when He falls into the earth and brings forth the fruit that the Father plans on bringing forth from His life, their hearts will have hope for change. Let me ask you a question today. What might be in your heart that would keep you from the greatest revival your life has ever seen? What stands in the way of your ministry, looking and acting like Jesus? What keeps you from help and change for your marriage, your finances or your relationship with others? Is it the mantle or covering you have been under for years? Whatever is keeping you from the surgery needed in your heart, whatever you might feel or think that is standing in the way of a fresh move of God in your life, release it. I pray that the intimacy that the Holy Spirit is drawing us into will produce what you need. The things that the Lord is after in our lives are the things that are trying to keep us from a fresh walk and awakening with Him. I pray that you will join a **"3rd Day"** savior in a **"3rd Day"** relationship.

Conclusion

It has always been a strong drive within me to see the church, the body of Christ, be all that God our Father has called us to be. I pray that this book has been a source of encouragement to you. I also believe that this book has prophetically placed our fingers on the pulse of what God is doing in our hearts. We must realize that God never showed up in any place or temple until the work was finished. The work that is taking place today is the calling and separation of a generation who wants more of Him. I encourage you to stay faithful to prayer and the strong preaching that comes from this intimacy. There are ministers all over America that are all saying, *"something must change."* Paul the Apostle warns us of a doctrine that would preach **another Jesus, a different Spirit, a different Gospel, and that it would be tolerated. (2 Corinthians 11:4)** I believe that it is not time to *"put up with it."* It's time to be fed up with it. There are men and women of God that are not concerned with being politically correct or socially acceptable, people who want to be Holy Spirit friendly, rather than seeker friendly, a people who want His presence more than the promises of His Word. We might be considered out dated and old fashion, but we still cling to what touches and fulfills man. The move of God will become popular again, and people will soon be seeking a people and a place that offers *Him.* He will show up in what He has prepared, a people who understands His hearts cry for them from the beginning. His presence and His glory are coming, stay Faithful brethren.

Dr. (Prophet) Tim Hines

An Exhortation of the 3rd Day
Dr. Don Hughes, Sr.

As we enter into *the "3rd Day"*, we are living in the time frame of the prophetic fulfillment of **(Daniel 12:9-12)**. In answer to Daniel's question "O my Lord, what shall be the end of these things?" The Lord's answer carries us off into this very day in which we are living.

"And he said go thy way, Daniel: for the words are closed up and sealed till the time of the end. *Many shall be purified, and made white and tried;* but the wicked shall do wickedly: and none of the wicked shall understand; but the wise shall understand."

We are living in the day of revelation. We are seeing the Word in a depth like no other generation. From the beginning of my ministry forty seven years at this writing – I have been interested in the studies of Biblical Numeric. This has carried over into the ministry of my son.

The Church is entering into its finest hour. The Spirit is being poured out upon all flesh **(Joel 2:28).** The Church must come out of its lukewarmness **(Rev. 3:16)** and experience a revival of holiness. The Lord promised the coming of the Great Teacher – The Holy Spirit.

"But the Comforter, which is the Holy Ghost, whom the Father will send in my name, he shall teach you all things, and bring all things to your remembrance, whatsoever I have said unto you: **(John 14:26)**. He is leading us into "all truth."

The above passage in Daniel makes another important statement that must be considered. ***"Many shall be purified and made white, and tried."*** The Church, for the most part, has slipped away from an intimate relationship with the Lord and into lukewarmness.

When Jesus was teaching His disciples on end time events, He said: "Watch therefore: for ye know not what hour your Lord doth come" **(Matt. 24:42)**, then two verses later He said **"Therefore be ye also ready..." (Vs. 44)**. It takes more than just "watching." You **MUST BE READY.** You cannot be lukewarm, neglecting the house of God and expect to be ready.

As we continue to read on into **Matthew Chapter Twenty-Five,** we find Ten Virgins. Five were wise and five were foolish. When the Lord returned, only those **"that were ready"** went into the marriage and the door was shut. The foolish were not ready and did not make it into the marriage feast. They were all virgins but just not all ready. **(Matt. 25:1-13).**

Listen to the words of Moses: "And the Lord said unto Moses, Go unto the people, and sanctify (separate unto holiness) them today (1000 years of the Church age – see **(I Peter 3:8)** and tomorrow (another 1000 years), and let them wash their clothes (notice they must clean up their lives before the Lord returns), AND BE READY AGAINST ***THE "3rd Day,"*** for ***the "3rd Day"*** the Lord will come down..." **(Exodus 19:10-11)** (My emphasis). This is the prophetic teaching of these verses.

Now we must ask that all important questions. What must we do to get ready? Part of the answer is to wash our clothes, which means to clean up our lives. The Lord gives us the rest of the answer: "who then is a faithful and wise servant, whom his lord hath made ruler over his household...Blessed is that servant, whom his lord when he cometh shall find so doing." **(Matt. 24:45-46).**

We must be found serving the Lord faithfully.

The book you have just read by my son, Apostle Don Hughes and Prophet Tim Hines is a masterful work on the subject of ***the "3rd Day"*** – truly it is the revealing of Christ in this earth.

The Lord is longsuffering, patient, kind, loving and merciful, giving everyone a chance to repent. He is looking for a Remnant who will make Him Lord of their lives. A Remnant of overcomers. A remnant who will obey His voice. All the promises given in the Word **will** come to pass. The Lord, through Peter said, in **(II Peter 3:11)**.

"Seeing then that all those things shall be dissolved, what manner of persons ought ye to be in all holy conversation and godliness."

Jesus said we must **"Be Ready" (Matthew 24:44; 25:10)** to be at His marriage supper.   **ARE YOU READY?**

Don Hughes Ministries
P.O. Box 840
Broken Arrow, OK 74013
Email:donhughesministries@cfaith.com
Website:www.donhughesministries.com

In his book, *Will The Spiritual Ones Please Come Forward,* Apostle Don Hughes shares the importance of restoring those who have "fallen away" from a biblical perspective.
$10.00

This powerful book is an eye-opener, it points out our responsibility in assisting and strengthening one another as we serve the Lord. Let's protect God's precious stones, don't let them fall through the spiritual cracks in the church and go unnoticed.
$10.00

Call or Write:

IMPACT Church

Apostle Don Hughes

P.O. Box 691563

Charlotte, NC 28227-7027

704-545-7579 Church office

704-545-9937 fax

www.impactchurchnc.org

email: apostledh@aol.com

Audio/Video/Book Order Form

Qty	Title	Price	Total
		Shipping & Handling	
		Grand Total	

Shipping & Handling Charges:

$5.00-$25.00 = $3.00 Shipping

$25.00-$75.00 =$5.00 Shipping

$75.00-$100.00 = $7.00 Shipping

Special discount for bulk orders, call

for pricing!

Payment Enclosed:

Check____   Money Order ____

Visa ____   Master Card ____

AMEX ____   Other ____

Credit Card # _____

Expiration Date _____

Signature _____

Name _____

Address_____

City_____ State _____

Zip _____

Send orders to:

Impact Church
P.O. Box 691563
Charlotte, NC 28227-7027

Fax orders:
704-545-9937

Email: apostledh@aol.com

Tim and Jodi Hines
P.O. Box 3416 Homosassa Springs, FL 34447 352-746-5308

Minister Order Form

Tapes:	Price	Order #:
1. A Process to His Presence (2 Tapes)	$10.00	A-1
2. Walking in love through Acceptance (2 Tapes)	$10.00	A-4
3. Hitting the Mark (2 Tapes)	$10.00	A-5
5. Rejoice, a Key to Revival, Restoration and Relationship (2 Tapes)	$10.00	A-6
5. Heavenly Economics (2 Tapes)	$10.00	A-7
6. Developing an Excellent Spirit (3 Tapes)	$15.00	A-9
7. The Family (3 Tapes)	$15.00	A-13
8. In the Secret Place (2 Tapes)	$10.00	A-17
9. Authority and the Anointing (2 Tapes)	$10.00	A-18

Please enclose $5.00 for shipping. Thank you

Order #: _____

Total: $ _____